The Secrets of
**SUCCESSFUL
HIRING
AND
FIRING**

Books in the series

The Secrets of Successful Business Letters
Clive Goodworth
The Secrets of Successful Copywriting Patrick Quinn
**The Secrets of Successful Low-budget
Advertising** Patrick Quinn
**The Secrets of Successful Sales
Management** Tony Adams
**The Secrets of Successful Speaking
and Business Presentations** Gordon Bell
The Secrets of Successful Selling Tony Adams

The Secrets of SUCCESSFUL HIRING AND FIRING

Clive T. Goodworth

Heinemann: London

Heinemann Professional Publishing Ltd
22 Bedford Square, London WC1B 3HH

LONDON   MELBOURNE
JOHANNESBURG   AUCKLAND

First published 1987

© Clive T. Goodworth 1987

British Library Cataloguing in Publication Data
Goodworth, Clive T.
The secrets of successful hiring and firing
1. Employees, Dismissal of – Great Britain
2. Recruiting of employees – Great Britain
I. Title
658.3'11'0941   HF5549.5.D55

ISBN 0 434 90678 6

Note: While every effort has been made to ensure the accuracy of the information and guidance contained within this book, no legal responsibility can, however, be accepted by the author or publisher for that information and guidance.

Photoset by Deltatype, Ellesmere Port
Printed in Great Britain by
Billings & Son Ltd, Worcester

Contents

List of figures   ix

Part One   *Hiring*

**1 Recruitment and selection – the essential
preamble**   3
An introductory chapter – a timely reminder
about the distinctly murky business of
recruitment and selection – coming to grips
with the job description and employee
specification – a bit on the theme of an overall
policy for recruitment and selection

2 Designing an effective application form   11
How not to design an application form – the all-
important employment history – the
'qualifications' bit – the education bit – the vexed
old 'hobbies' bit – the ubiquitous '$64,000
question' bit – medical questionnaires – the
hallowed business of references

**3 All about recruitment sources and
advertisements**   33
Sources of recruitment: playing the incest game –

vi *Contents*

what about Job Centres? – what-ho for the Professional and Executive Register. *Effective recruitment advertising*: the aims – obtaining an appropriate response – providing a clear, concise and attractive description of the post – the scran-bag of recruitment advertisers' flannel and how to avoid it – enhancing the company image – the four 'rights' of recruitment advertising – 'blinkered' ads – a 'dial-an-ad' phrase bank – a note on discrimination

4 Short-listing and interview techniques 53
A warning preamble – coping with the short list – rejecting them nicely – preparing for the fray – a checklist on the interview environment – a self-questionnaire on interviewing skills and aptitudes – planning the interview – the technique of asking questions in the right way – an interview sampler – a post-interview assessment procedure

5 Processing the lucky ones 89
The written offer of employment – written statements of particulars of employment – contracts of employment – probation is all about being fair – they call it induction training

Part Two Firing

6 Dismissal – another essential preamble 99
A preamble on some bad attitudes to dismissal and an introduction to the only *good* attitude – tips for checking a disciplinary procedure – periods of notice – something on constructive dismissal – suspension

Contents vii

7 Dismissing the baddies and the failures 109
Dismissal for misconduct: some questions and answers – practical tips on dealing with cases of gross misconduct – dismissal for 'totted-up' offences – the paperwork for warnings and dismissal for misconduct. *Dismissal related to capability and/or qualifications*: dealing with such cases – the associated paperwork for warnings and dismissal – probation – incapability and dismissal through ill-health

8 Redundancy 133
The basic definition – the duty to *avoid* redundancies – entitlements to redundancy payments – the requirement to consult trade unions – consultation in 'non-union' situations – notifying planned redundancies to the Department of Employment – selecting for redundancy – time off for job-hunting and to arrange training – redundancy dismissal letters – resolving queries – a summary of unfair dismissal for redundancy

9 Dismissal hiccups and treading the tribunal trail 149
Written statements of reasons for dismissal – references in general – references and the Rehabilitation of Offenders Act 1974 – *Facing an industrial tribunal – and surviving*: initial action on receiving a complaint – using the Conciliation Officer – preparing for the fray – the tribunal setting dissected – presenting and hopefully winning one's case

viii   *Contents*

Appendices

1 Example of an application for employment designed for use in the recruitment of clerical and other junior staff   172

Example of an application for employment designed for use in management recruitment   182

2 Example of a written statement of particulars of employment   183

Recommended reading list   185

Index   187

Figures

Figure	1	*A positively striking example of how* not *to design an application form*	13
Figure	2	*Another employer's stab at investigating a candidate's employment history*	17
Figure	3	*A mythical candidate's completion of the employment history illustrated in Figure 2*	18
Figure	4	*An adequate example of an employment history section for operative (etc.)/supervisory-level recruitment*	20
Figure	5	*An example of part of an employment history section in an application form designed for executive recruitment*	21
Figure	6	*An example of a qualifications (etc.) section of an application form*	23
Figure	7	*An example of an education section*	24
Figure	8	*An example of a 'hobbies and leisure pursuits' section*	26
Figure	9	*A medical questionnaire that enjoys pride of place in the Goodworth Black Museum*	28
Figure	10	*A typical formal warning in respect of misconduct*	117
Figure	11	*A typical final warning in respect of misconduct*	118

x *Figures*

Figure 12 *A typical notification of summary dismissal for misconduct* 120

Figure 13 *A typical warning in respect of incapability* 123

Figure 14 *Example of skeleton dismissal notice for incapability* 125

Figure 15 *A skeleton letter of dismissal on redundancy* 142

Part One Hiring

1 Recruitment and selection – the essential preamble

In other words, getting your act together

For starters, what about a hearty gnaw on a thigh-sized bone of contention? Here we go, then – it's simply that, of all the managers at the sharp end of business and industry who are lumbered with the task of hiring people, only around a miserable 5 per cent have received any worthwhile training in the art. Or, to put it another way, while an army of Big Daddies continue to bolster their annual reports with such euphemistic phrases as 'our employees are our most valuable asset', the hard truth is that the vast majority of their executive minions are shockingly ill-equipped to select these much-vaunted treasures.

Lest you doubt this, consider the question of company training, in general. When, as often happens, a manager is faced with a new process, or whatever, which affects the 'technical' side of his or her job, it's a pretty fair bet that the overworked creature will be quickly despatched on a suitable course. But, and here's the tragic rub, when it comes to equipping Jack or Jill Executive with an insight into the equally important aspects of 'general' management, what usually happens? Why, me hearty, precisely nothing. In the eyes of umpteen employers, formal training in such antics is strictly for the birds – and woe betide the seeker-of-knowledge who has the temerity to suggest

4 The Secrets of Successful Hiring and Firing

otherwise. Come to think of it, Big Daddy's battle-cry has a terribly familiar ring – 'Look, Smithers, you're a manager now, so just get out there – and manage. . . .'

Ramming my opening point home, far too many employers seem to believe that the very act of spawning a new manager is a sure-fire signal for the Great Chairman in the Sky to reach down and inject the poor so-and-so with, among myriad other qualities, pure essence of interviewing skills.

Since, unhappily, such divine intervention is normally conspicuous by its absence, it follows that umpteen victims of management apathy are simply left to muddle through this vital, square-one process of sorting the candidate wheat from the chaff.

> *'Muddle through, d'you say? Hey, man, that's a bit strong. . . . I may not've had any formal training, but I reckon I'm as good an interviewer as the next man. . . . Put it this way, I've hired quite a few people in my time – and I haven't dropped that many clangers. . .'.*

If that is your reaction, good on you – I can't honestly admit to much surprise. After all said and done, you've spent goodness knows how many years mingling and speaking with people – and, surely, all the wisdom and experience you've thus accrued must count for something, mustn't it? To say the least, it's not very nice when this flamin' book-wallah has the temerity to poke his finger in your ribs and suggest that, as a hirer of people, you'd make a good gardener. . . . However, be a devil and bear with me while we take a swift gander at – hell, what's in a name, let's call it

THE HIRING PROCESS – A MINI-CATALOGUE OF WARTS

Wart No. 1 'Job descriptions are a waste of time'
I'm not really a gambler at heart, but I'm willing to bet anything you like that if I round up a bevy of managers and,

Recruitment and selection – the essential preamble 5

having pinned 'em to the wall, pose the round-robin question, 'Now, Honest Injun, how many of you make use of job descriptions when hiring people?', I'll get a pretty mucky response.

'Er, 'scuse me, but what's a job description, loike?'

(Oh, yes, you'd better believe it – there are those managers who've never even heard of them.)

'Hum, I do believe I remember seeing one of those once – now, when was it?'

'We've certainly got job descriptions. . . . At least, I know I've got one – t'was issued six years ago when I joined the company. But they're never used for anything, let alone hiring people. . . . I think it was the Industrial Training Board who insisted that they had to be drawn up – something to do with qualifying for grants, or what-not. . . .'

'Why on earth d'you need a job description when filling a vacancy? Any manager worth his salt knows exactly what's entailed in the job concerned – it's just another example of blinkin' bureaucracy gone mad, that's what it is. . . .'

And so on.

I hope you'll agree, reader, that, whatever the size of the firm concerned, each and every employee is entitled to have a formal *and* up-to-date statement of the purpose and duties of his or her job. If only for this reason, it behoves us to familiarize ourselves with the layout of a typical job description:

Job identification
The job title, its location, etc.

The purpose of the job
A statement of the primary objectives of the job.

6 The Secrets of Successful Hiring and Firing

The duties of the job

A list of the duties and tasks involved.

Responsibilities of the job

A precise statement of the responsibilities involved, expressed in terms of people, money, equipment, etc.

Relationships

A precise statement of the working relationships involved in the job.

Terms and conditions

Details of pay and other entitlements, hours of work, etc.

But it goes further than merely producing a piece of paper for the employee's benefit, important though that is. Like it or not, the job description is an essential adjunct to management, in general – and to the hiring process, in particular. In order to understand why this is so, it's necessary to consider the next wart in our catalogue of hiring ills.

Wart No. 2 'Employee specifications – they're a waste of time, as well'

I won't bore you rigid with the catechism of reactions by far too many managers to the question of employee specifications. Suffice it to say that these ain't exactly top of the executive hit parade, either – which is little short of scandalous. I'm probably teaching you to suck eggs, but it's got to be said – the employee specification (yes, that's right, it's based on the job description) is a formal statement of the personal characteristics, qualities and qualifications required in applicants for the job concerned. In other words, *it's nothing less than the blueprint of the ideal candidate for the job.* Once the requirements for a particular job have been established, the wise manager will take things a stage

Recruitment and selection – the essential preamble 7

further and quantify these criteria under the headings 'essential' and 'desirable', as in this example:

	Essential	Desirable
Posting of sales ledger	Arithmetical skill (GCSE, etc.)	Familarity with invoices, cheques, credit notes. Ability to produce analysis heads.

To neglect the colossal importance of the job description and employee specification in the hiring scheme of things is to invite disaster.

JOB DESCRIPTION

Compiling a job description does not mean merely sitting at your desk and indulging in a spot of literary fantasy. The name of the game is job analysis – and that entails a *detailed study* of the job

EMPLOYEE SPECIFICATION

Based on the job description, the 'candidate criteria' must be *realistic* – you don't stand much chance of recruiting Superman, so refrain from the temptation to describe him in your employee specification

JOB ADVERTISEMENT

Use the job description and employee specification as vital sources of reference when compiling that compellingly attractive advertisement. . . .

CANDIDATE SELECTION

And, also, when you are selecting the pick of the bunch

8 *The Secrets of Successful Hiring and Firing*

Wart No. 3 The big yin: 'Look, we've been hiring people for years – so why all the fuss, eh?'
Yes, you're right, this is where we came in. However, in turning my introductory wheel full circle, it's only right that I should cap my opening indictment with some constructive stuff – so, having hopefully convinced you that job descriptions and employee specifications are vital necessities, here are some ground rules for the formulation of an overall policy for company recruitment and selection.

1 Policies flow from those high-flying things, objectives – the goals to be sought – and any policy for hiring people should first define its aim; for example: *to devise and maintain the highest standards of recruitment and selection of the human resources required by the company to achieve its primary objectives.*

2 It's all too easy for any manager to select a poor candidate for a job if, as is so often the case, the hapless creature's been clobbered right from the start with a second-rate bunch of applicants. Hence, if you will, the pundits' resounding emphasis on effective *recruitment.* Think in terms of recruitment policy – and your thoughts must surely turn to application forms and advertising.

Application forms. Despite the fact that the application form is one of the most important pieces of boomph in the company stationery store, it's more than likely that it represents the dubious product of precious little thought. Ergo, ensure that your policy embraces the crucial need for good quality documentation – and, hopefully, the nitty-gritty tips in Chapter 2 will help you to fulfil this need.

Advertising. Look at it this way, if the executive wallahs in almost any run-of-the-mill company worked one-tenth as hard on the design and content of their

Recruitment and selection – the essential preamble 9

recruiting ads as they usually do on their marketing publicity, it's on the cards that they'd be up to the gunnels in suitable candidates. If the implied cap fits, don't just wear it – carry on with your policy renovation, and dig into Chapter 3.

3   And now for the *selection* chunk of the policy, the dreaded short-listing and interviewing processes. Albeit that Chapter 4 sets out to provide some assistance in navigating these murky waters, there can be no substitute for good, sound training in selection techniques – and your policy should reflect and emphasize this overriding requirement. But, be warned, there are many cowboy outfits who've hitched a ride on the training band-wagon; so, before you succumb to their tempting blandishments regarding this or that course on selection, seek the advice of the professionals – the British Institute of Management, the Institute of Personnel Management, or other with-it body.

4   No decent policy on hiring employees would be complete without reference to that bugbear of sharp-end administrators, the initial employment-cum-induction paperwork. The aim of Chapter 5 is to steer you clear of the salient dangers in this particular minefield – which, as the Industrial Tribunals constantly remind us, has been responsible for the premature demise of many a manager. . . .

I reckon that's just about enough for the prologue. Hullo, reader, and welcome – let's get the show on the road.

2   Designing an effective application form

Or, if you prefer it, how not to commit harakiri

Before tackling this chapter, I'd like you to pop into the outer office, or wherever, and seek out a copy of your company's application form. It may well be, of course, that you utilize more than one version; if so, get copies of them all – the more the merrier. Thus armed, you'll be able to compare your firm's efforts with the various bits and pieces that I'm going to offer for your inspection – and, who knows, you may even come up smelling of violets!

But before we plunge into the mechanics of application form design, I'm afraid it's necessary to touch on the dreaded legal aspects – for, like it or not, in this country, the Commission for Racial Equality and the Equal Opportunities Commission have both had their say in relation to applications for employment.

SO WHERE'S THE CATCH?

In short, the answer to that thorny question is the potential Sword of Damocles that hangs over the head of anyone who sets out to design an application form without due regard for the legal implications involved. For example,

12   *The Secrets of Successful Hiring and Firing*

employers have a *penchant* for including 'place of birth' within the make-up of the application – information which cannot be labelled, or so we are told, as vital or even necessary to the selection process.

In the UK, the thinking manager who wishes to avoid, or, at the very least, make himself aware of the legal pitfalls inherent in recruitment and selection (including application form design) should make it his business to acquire copies of:

(a)   The Code of Practice issued by the Commission for Racial Equality for the elimination of racial discrimination and the promotion of equal opportunity in employment.

(b)   The Code of Practice issued by the Equal Opportunities Commission for the elimination of discrimination on the grounds of sex and marriage (note, please – *and marriage*) and the promotion of equal opportunity in employment.

One general rule is that application forms should not require information to be supplied which can seem discriminatory to those candidates who fail at the short-listing stage. Having stated thus, I am acutely aware that I've disturbed a likely hornets' nest, but there it is.

HOW NOT TO DESIGN AN APPLICATION FORM

First, there's a most important homily to be preached – and take my word for it, you ignore it at your peril!

AN APPLICATION FORM THAT POSES PEANUT-TYPE QUESTIONS CANNOT FAIL TO PRODUCE MONKEY-TYPE ANSWERS

Although it's blatantly obvious that a poorly designed form will throw a damned great spanner in the short-listing

Designing an effective application form   13

ANONYMOUS LTD

APPLICATION FOR EMPLOYMENT

Surname ....   Christian names ....

Address ....

....   Tel no. ....

Age ....   Date and place of birth ....

Nationality ....

Details of person to contact in case of emergency ....

....

What prompted this application? ....

What position do you seek? ....

Present employer? ....

May we contact your present employer? ....

Postion held ....   Wage/salary ....

Reason for leaving ....

Please list any serious operations or illnesses ....

....

Disability, if any ....   Reg. disability no. ....

Education and qualifications ....

....

....

Signed ....   Date ....

For office use only

Interviewed by ....   Date ....

Accepted/Rejected   Starting date ....

Figure 1   *A positively striking example of how* not *to design an application form*

14 *The Secrets of Successful Hiring and Firing*

works, very few organizations give more than a passing thought to this fact of selection life. While this is particularly true of the small firm (where, let's face it, hiring the right people is, if anything, even more crucial to success), umpteen quite sizeable companies are tarred with the same nasty brush.

Take a long, hard look at Figure 1 – which, incidentally, is a copy of the 'typed and duplicated' application form sported by a Cambridgeshire engineering outfit with over 200 employees. No matter what the vacancy, be it management or shop floor, this is the horror that confronts each and every applicant. See what you think of it. . . .

Yes, you're right – a pretty horrible form. Let's just note some of its more outstanding faults:

- The attempt to secure information on a candidate's current or latest employment is little more than a travesty of investigative questioning. Needless to say, we'll be concentrating on this aspect a bit later on.

- As if intent on compounding this initial sin, the unknown compiler has omitted any reference at all to the candidate's *previous* employment. On these first two counts alone, the company would be well advised to commit selection suicide, for their poor old shortlisters cannot be expected to survive such a dearth of essential information.

- Almost adding insult to injury, the form is peppered with what can only be construed as puerile attempts to introduce a note of 'expertise' into the text:

  'Details of person to contact in case of emergency'

  Lest you have doubts over this point (mind you, I'm sure you don't), why in blazes does the company need to know details of next-of-kin at this early stage in the game? Oh, I don't know – perhaps they've had some unfortunate candidate drop dead on them at interview.

Designing an effective application form 15

'What prompted this application?'

When used in the context of a properly designed form, there's nothing wrong with this type of question – but we're dealing with an *improperly* designed example. The thing is, so much else has been omitted that it's inclusion sticks out like a sore thumb – providing us with a crystal-clear indication that the compiler's priorities were way up the creek. In addition, and if we're to be wholly destructive in our criticism, the question is badly worded – facetious though it may be, a courageous Joe Soap really couldn't be blamed if he responded, 'Hunger, you idiot. . . .'

'What position do you seek?'

Again, when examined in isolation, the question is quite legitimate. However, its particular location in this form, halfway down the page, provides a cogent clue to the compiler's approach – an unconsidered slapping-down of items as and when they came to mind, with little or no planning for logicality, purpose or effect.

● The stark words, 'Education and qualifications', exert no control over the candidate, in that the question is far too open-ended, inviting nothing but a mish-mash of information in response.

To sum up the all-too-obvious, the form is a failure. There is simply no way in which it can require a candidate to provide a comprehensive account of past experience-cum-achievement – and, as a consequence, the company just has to tumble head-over-heels at this first fence in the selection handicap.

Er, sorry – what was that?

'Look, Goodworth, or whatever your name is – don't get too carried away. . . . Most of my recruiting's at shop floor level, taking on production workers – and no one's going to

convince me that you need a bloody great long, super-detailed application form for that kind of recruitment. . . . If they can do the job that's required of 'em and haven't been in trouble, if they look okay at interview – well, they're in. It's as simple as that. . . . Good grief, man, we haven't got the time to indulge in all this sophisticated stuff – and, as I've said, it's just not necessary, anyway.'

Aha, things are getting lively. . . . It's certainly a fact that one doesn't need (to use your possible words) a bloody great long, super-detailed application form when recruiting shop floor workers. But, me hearty, let me tell you what you *do* need – a shorter form, maybe, *but it's just got to be one that poses the right questions.*

And that's what this chapter is all about.

THE ALL-IMPORTANT EMPLOYMENT HISTORY

Let's take another look at the 'employment bit' in that form depicted in Figure 1:

Present employer? ....

May we contact your present employer? ....

Position held .... Wage/salary ....

Reason for leaving ....

Now, if you will, compare the dearth of detail with that in the example in Figure 2 – culled from one of the exhibits in my application form scrapbook.

Plainly, the example in Figure 2 represents a considerable improvement. The compiler has not only catered for the current/most recent post held, but has also included a section on prior employment – ergo, at the very least, we have a mini-dossier in the making.

Designing an effective application form 17

EMPLOYMENT HISTORY

Current/last employer .... Business ....

Address ....

Post held .... From .... To ....

Duties ....

Starting pay .... Present/leaving pay ....

Reason for leaving/wish to leave ....

Please give details of your previous employment, beginning with the most recent.

Employer .... Business ....

Address ....

Post held .... From .... To ....

Leaving pay .... Reason for leaving ....

Employer .... Business ....

Address ....

Post held .... From ....

Figure 2 *Another employer's stab at investigating a candidate's employment history*

So, you may ask, what's wrong with it? Ah, well, in answer to that one, let's get a mythical candidate to plonk his job-seeking pen to paper. . . .

18 *The Secrets of Successful Hiring and Firing*

EMPLOYMENT HISTORY

Current/~~last~~ employer ~~ECTISLEY PRODUCS~~ Business ~~AUTOMOTIVE~~
   CURRENT   LTD   PARTS

Address ~~UNIT 4b, EASTWOOD PARK IND. EST. PETERBOROUGH~~

Post held ~~SUPERVISOR~~ From ~~AUG 1983~~ To ~~MAY 1986~~
   PRODUCTION

Duties ~~SUPERVISION OF SHIFT WORKERS IN SHOCK ABSORBER~~
   PRODUCTION SHOP

Starting pay ~~£2.15 per hr~~ Present/leaving pay ~~£2.80 p/hr plus~~
   shift bonus

~~Reason for leaving~~/wish to leave ~~TO SEEK BETTER POSITION~~

Please give details of your previous employment, beginning with the
most recent.

Employer ~~BROOKES LTD~~ Business ~~ELECTRICAL ACCESSORIES~~

Address ~~LEYTON INDUSTRIAL ESTATE, BROWNHILLS,~~
   ~~DUNSTABLE, BEDS~~

Post held ~~COIL ASSEMBLY CHARGEHAND~~ From ~~JAN 1980~~ To ~~AUG 1983~~

Leaving pay ~~£1.40 per hr~~ Reason for leaving ~~MOVE TO~~
   + overtime and shift   PETERBOROUGH
   rate

Employer ~~LINK MANUFACTURE LTD~~ Business ~~MILK FLOAT MANUFACTURERS~~

Address ~~LINK WORKS, THUNDERSLEY, ESSEX~~

Post held ~~CHARGEHAND~~ From ~~1973~~

Figure 3 *A mythical candidate's completion of the employment
history illustrated in Figure 2*

The point is, Figure 3 depicts one of the most common
weaknesses to be found in *any* forms, let alone applications
for employment – totally inadequate space for the required
entries. Even if it does mean expanding the most basic of

Designing an effective application form 19

forms to cover both sides of an A4 sheet – why, for goodness sake, do so. Think again of the short-listing process – of the immense difficulties inherent in thumbing through a pile of applications, and trying with little success to compare crammed-in, squashed-up bits of information.

Hum, do I sense another comment?

'Too right, you do. . . . Isn't it time that you stopped teaching me to suck eggs – and, just for a change, got round to something useful in the way of help?'

Well, guess what, I have no intention of apologizing. While I've nothing but praise for your self-professed ability to cover all the 'basics' without this author-chappie laying down the law, there's a whole army of managers who fail to match your proficiency – and that's a fact. So, be a devil, give yourself a mighty pat on the back and bide with me – if only to confirm that you really are the bee's knees where application forms are concerned. . . .

Oh, yes – and stand by for a further opportunity to mutter, 'Here we go, again. . . .' Figure 4 illustrates a typically adequate layout for the employment history section of a form for use in operative (etc.)/supervisory recruitment. We'll deal with its management-level counterpart in a tick.

When casting around for management-type candidates, it is even more important that application forms encourage – nay, literally force – aspiring applicants to present fulsome and near-accurate accounts of their respective backgrounds. I use the term 'near-accurate' advisedly, for it is an unfortunate fact of selection life that about 40 per cent of the information supplied in application forms is *in*accurate. This is not to say that candidates lie in their teeth (although some of the beggars do) but, rather, that they engage in the time-honoured and quite natural art of 'embroidery'. Think on it, did *you* not dress up your last application to the very best of your creative ability, and didn't this sweaty effort

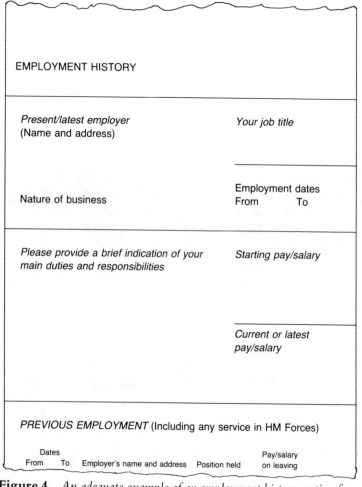

Figure 4 *An adequate example of an employment history section for operative (etc.)/supervisory-level recruitment*

include a healthy dollop of embroidery?

So, in an effort to arrive at the near-truth, an application form for executive employment should contain some additional, more pointed requests for information – and Figure 5 provides an illustration of what I mean.

Designing an effective application form   21

CURRENT/LATEST EMPLOYMENT

Name and address of employer

Your job title

Nature of business

Employment dates

From   To

To whom responsible
(Name and job title)

Salary on Joining

Current/latest salary

How many people report(ed) directly
to you? (Give job titles)

Details of fringe benefits

How many people are/were in your
overall control? (Detail by numbers and
sections, etc.)

If still in post, what
period of notice are you
required to give?

22   *The Secrets of Successful Hiring and Firing*

Please provide a brief but concise description of your main duties and responsibilities. Kindly indicate, by means of an organization diagram, your position in the company.

Figure 5   *An example of part of an employment history section in an application form designed for executive recruitment*

THE 'QUALIFICATIONS' BIT

Continuing the jolly old theme that, if one asks peanut-type questions within the application form, one is bound to get monkey-type answers, it's plain that we must give some attention to the section dealing with qualifications – so let's do just that.

There's no finer way to start than to remind you that the crux of the selection game is *caveat emptor* – and, application form-wise, one of the biggest potential minefields is the section dealing with qualifications. Leaping on a bit, and believe it or not, with the possible exception of applications for employment from school-leavers, very few run-of-the-mill employers ever ask to view candidates' certificates or diplomas – and, incredibly, this is even more true where degree parchments are concerned. In fact, the average Big Daddy wouldn't even recognize a degree parchment if he saw one. With this salient failing in mind, it behoves us to ensure that, at the very least, our application forms reflect a modicum of care when requesting such details.

Have a cup of coffee, and then take a crafty gander at Figure 6.

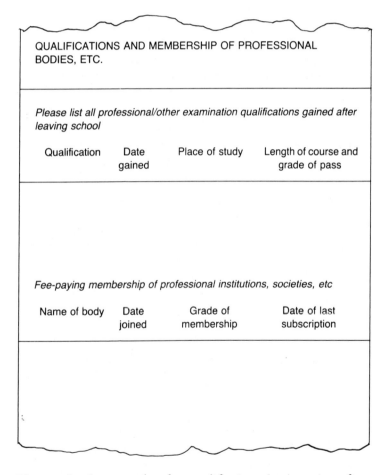

Figure 6 *An example of a qualifications (etc.) section of an application form*

As you will have gathered, the object of the section illustrated in Figure 6 is to sort out the 'qualifications' wheat from the chaff. For instance, it is useful to know that a candidate who is an Associate Member, say, of the Institution of Industrial Managers qualified for such membership by successfully completing a two-year, part-time course at college – instead of merely becoming a member in return for a few quid. Obviously, such a qualification would be reflected by an entry in both parts of the section; provided, of course, that the applicant was completely honest regarding his or her annual subscription. The

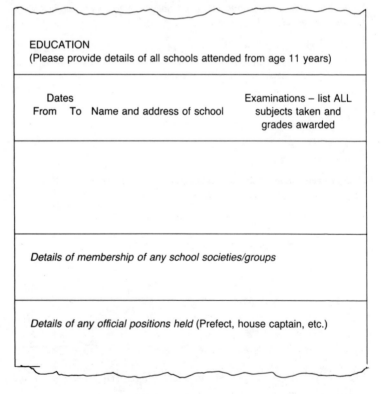

Figure 7 *An example of an education section*

management world is full to overflowing with lapsed members of this or that institution; and, while you may not deem it of world-shaking importance, it's a good idea to discourage fibbing where possible – hence the 'date of last subscription' column.

THE EDUCATION BIT

While a grizzly, middle-aged veteran may feel with some justification that being required to dig up details of schooling is a bit much, if the form is to be utilized for recruiting young applicants, an education section is absolutely essential. Anyway, what's wrong with making the older person do a spot of memory-jogging – and thus complete his or her pen-picture?

So, eyes down and looking at Figure 7. . . .

Note that, although the example in Figure 7 requires all examination subjects to be listed, it makes no actual mention of the word 'failures'. Again, it may seem like nit-picking, but there is a highly emotive ring to the term and it is best omitted. Stating the requirement as it does, the form plainly relies on the applicant's complete honesty – but, after all, when appropriate, the subject of a candidate's educational successes and failures should receive full treatment at the interview stage.

THE VEXED OLD 'HOBBIES' BIT

Since we're going to dwell on the question of candidates' leisure activities in a later chapter, suffice it to comment at this stage that the winner-applicant for any job is (or damned well should be) the best-qualified person – and one such *essential* qualification is that good old proverbial attribute, fire in the belly. The candidate who switches off at cease-work and becomes a TV-addicted vegetable, or what-not, for the rest of his or her time, will possess nary a

26 The Secrets of Successful Hiring and Firing

flicker – and the application form just has to provide the short-lister with at least some clues on this vital aspect.

HOBBIES AND OTHER INTERESTS

When listing your hobbies and other interests, kindly indicate the type and depth of your involvement in each activity (Time spent; whether a casual or serious pursuit; achievements; positions held in teams, clubs; etc.)

Figure 8 *An example of a 'hobbies and leisure pursuits' section*

A bald, unqualified request for information on extra-mural activities merely invites casual completion, so give applicants a challenge – in other words, make them think about the topic.

THE UBIQUITOUS '$64,000 QUESTION' BIT

When seeking to recruit for management posts, many eager employers are drawn like honey-bees to the heady scent of the 'test the blighter to death' type question. While most of these hardy perennials bloom during the interview, the application form doesn't exactly escape scot-free; for example:

'What position do you wish to hold in 5–10 years' time, and how do you plan to achieve this goal?'

'Provide a brief but succinct account of your medium- and long-term career objectives.'

Designing an effective application form 27

'Please enter any additional information about yourself which you think will help us to assess your suitability for employment with Gubbins Ltd.'

And, of course, the real corker:

'Why are you applying for this post?' (*Usually followed by six blood-curdling inches of blank space.*)

All right then – so what is wrong with these much-beloved $64,000 questions? The short answer is quite a lot, namely:

(a) They are intensely subjective – and, used within a process which is already knee-deep in subjectivity, they merely add to the tarnish.

(b) It follows from (a) that each such question has no truly 'correct answer.' *Every lip-smacking short-lister will have his or her firmly-held views on what constitutes a good response* – but, believe me, that's a very different kettle of fish. The unpalatable fact is that very few of us are genuinely qualified to assess what candidates have to say in reply to these beasties; except, perhaps, in terms of powers of written expression.

However, I'm quite sure that my single cry in the wilderness will have absolutely no effect. There are very few of us who do not enjoy a profound self-esteem where the ability to judge other people is concerned – and this 'I know a good chap when I see one' syndrome is equally pronounced when it comes to assessing their written narratives. What more can I say?

DRAWING THE STRINGS TOGETHER

Very hopefully, having examined all the 'primary' sections of an application form, you will now be in a position to decide whether or not you need to amend or rehash your own masterpiece(s). As a small recompense for dutifully

28 The Secrets of Successful Hiring and Firing

ploughing through this chapter (and in order to save you some work), Appendix 1 provides a couple of complete forms for your consideration – so, more power to your application-designing elbow!

MEDICAL QUESTIONNAIRE

Have you ever suffered from/received treatment for any of the following? (Delete where applicable)

Asthma	Yes/No	Back strain	Yes/No
Hay fever	Yes/No	Disc trouble	Yes/No
Diabetes	Yes/No	Arthritis	Yes/No
Jaundice	Yes/No	Rheumatism	Yes/No
Rupture	Yes/No	Chest pain	Yes/No
Stomach/intestinal ulcer	Yes/No	Heart murmur	Yes/No
Convulsions or fits	Yes/No	Heart attack	Yes/No
Tuberculosis	Yes/No	Kidney disease	Yes/No
Pneumonia	Yes/No	Gallstone	Yes/No
Ear trouble	Yes/No	High blood pressure	Yes/No
Fainting spells	Yes/No	Shortness of breath	Yes/No
Eye trouble	Yes/No	Bronchitis	Yes/No
Rheumatic fever	Yes/No	Chronic cough	Yes/No
Varicose veins	Yes/No	Nervous breakdown	Yes/No

Have you ever had any other serious illness or surgical operation? (Give details)

Do you have any physical defects or disability(Give details)

I certify that I have answered this questionnaire correctly and that, to the best of my knowledge, the answers I have provided are true in every detail.

Signature .... Date ....

Figure 9 *A medical questionnaire that enjoys pride of place in the Goodworth Black Museum*

SOME ADDITIONAL BITS AN' BOBS

MEDICAL QUESTIONNAIRES

Many organizations require applicants to provide some indication of their medical history and, in a flush of enthusiasm, include questions on the subject somewhere within their application paraphernalia. Unfortunately, only a few employers take the trouble to consult a doctor on what should, or should not be included in such questionnaires – and, boy, the results can be quite horrific. See what you think of the example in Figure 9.

Merely looking at Figure 9 makes me feel queasy. . . . The moral must be, if you do utilize medical questionnaires of any shape or size, do ensure that they have your company quack's approval.

THE HALLOWED BUSINESS OF REFERENCES

By all means, include within the application form a statement to the effect that, subject to the applicant's permission, employers' references will be obtained – but *never* succumb to using anything like the following requirement:

> 'Please supply the names and addresses of two persons (including your present employer) to whom reference can be made in connection with this application.'

This is a standing invitation to an applicant to enlist the services of his or her best pal or the next-door neighbour in coming up trumps with a sparkling, combined effort, second reference. You know it and I know it – so why the hell do so many employers still perpetrate this idiotic practice?

Pardon me, but your slip is showing

A well-designed application form not only increases the chances of short-listing success, *it also enhances the company image*. It's wise to remember that rejected applicants for employment may need very little encouragement to become the firm's worst ambassadors – and a grotty, amateurish application form could well be the spur to stacks of denigrating and swiftly-spreading comment.

I reckon you've earned a breather. . . .

3 All about recruitment sources and advertisements
Wanted yesterday – a miracle . . .

If, as we're constantly reminded by a horde of pontificating bosses, an organization's people are its most valuable asset, it seems little short of tragic that so many of these self-same employers look upon recruitment as a kind of hit-or-miss, flap-activity – to be conducted with minimal planning and, as near as dammit, on a shoestring budget. This is particularly the case where recruitment advertising is concerned, but before we grapple with that thorny aspect, we'd better kick off from square-one, as it were – and take a look at some likely sources of applicants.

PLAYING THE INCEST GAME

The other day, I happened to visit a company whose proud boast is that, whenever they're in the market for new people, they always endeavour to recruit relatives and friends of their existing employees. Their creed is simple and, on the surface, attractive:

- The method, they say, is highly economic – since, quite obviously, there's no need to spend money on expensive advertising and other trawling activities.
- Because their employees invariably have a good idea

34 *The Secrets of Successful Hiring and Firing*

what will be required of applicants for this or that job, the management is often presented with a ready-made short list – and, ho, ho, what could be better?

● Last but not least, because an employee would never dream of recommending someone he or she disliked, the method ensured that the company was a friendly place in which to work.

Now, there's precious little doubt that the recruitment of pals and relatives of staff is dirt-cheap – and, in all probability, pleases both those who do the introducing and, not unnaturally, those who are thus taken into the fold. But it does expose the unwary boss to at least a couple of weighty risks:

1 Because the organization is often presented with a ready-made short list (in many instances, it's a 'short list' of one), the very process of selection suffers erosion from the start. The trouble is, your average manager will be more inclined to accept Joe Operative's word that cousin George is a rattling good chap than set about the difficult task of establishing the truth himself. Plainly, while such personal recommendations can and do pay off on the odd, fortunate occasion, they should never be utilized as an invariable excuse for handy selection short-cuts.

2 You won't need reminding that one of the reasons why incest is taboo is because it leads messily to in-breeding – and recruitment incest is no exception. All right, it would be a gross exaggeration to offer that hiring employee-recommended people is tantamount to cloning one's workforce, but the guys and gals of the outfit *will* be inclined to recruit in their own image – which is all hunky-dory, provided that they, themselves, are without undue blemish. And, even if the method doesn't result in an increasing number of rotten apples in the barrel, it's well on the cards (especially in

the case of the small company) that a cosy, family-type atmosphere will develop – and, contrary to popular belief, this won't exactly enhance the maintenance of discipline *or* production.

We should also remember that a number of organizations make one hell of a fetish of *promoting* from within. And, would you believe, some of them have the temerity to argue that 'the demoralizing effect of bringing in outsiders' far outweighs any hazard of in-breeding. Quite apart from stinking to high heaven of 22-carat paternalism, this nasty addiction cannot fail to starve the corporate life-blood of its vital red corpuscles – and anaemic in-breeding is no longer a mere hazard, it becomes a brass-bound, fatal certainty. Sure, promoting one's own people is cheap, often effective and, sometimes, good for morale – but the message must be, moderation in all things. All organizations thrive on fresh air, so keep those recruitment windows open. . . .

WHAT ABOUT JOB CENTRES?

Quiz any manager on the efficacy of Job Centres as a source of recruitment, and it's more than likely that his response will be less than lukewarm. Certainly, in my experience, it seems the case that, while a minority of employers utilize this government agency as a fair to middlin' source of operative-cum-clerical recruitment, the vast remainder regard the services offered by Job Centres with an acutely jaundiced eye.

In the event that you agree with this sweeping generalization, hearken ye to one man's tale of success. . . . An employer-friend of mine who, in the words of the poet, 'had had it up to here' where the ineffectiveness of his local Job Centre was concerned, decided that he wouldn't let this particular sleeping dog lie. Finding it necessary to recruit new, middle-of-the-road people, he started off by remind-

36   *The Secrets of Successful Hiring and Firing*

ing the local Job Centre *supremo* of the one reason for the Department's existence – to provide a free and comprehensive service for the recruitment of staff with a wide range of abilities and skills. He then clambered on the guy's back – and proceeded to chivvy him unmercifully until such time as he was satisfied that he was receiving an acceptable standard of service. He didn't impose excessive or unrealistic demands, you understand, but merely ensured that the Job Centre came up to scratch – for, to quote his own words, 'Why should an employer spend hard-earned money on recruitment when he's already paying a government outfit to do the self-same thing?'

And he's got a point. . . . If you don't already do so, start to make use of your Job Centre, and if they fail to toe the line where your moderate requirements are concerned, thump them – and thump them hard. Commit to mind the fact that we reap the Civil Service that we deserve – and, if you still need some encouragement to get off your butt, just take a glance at your tax bill.

WHAT-HO FOR THE PROFESSIONAL AND EXECUTIVE REGISTER . . .

The PER (the 'quality end' of the Manpower Services Commission's hierarchy of aids for the unemployed) may well be able to help out with the recruitment of managers and specialists – and while, as you may know, their service isn't free to employers, it represents very good value for money. If you want your advertisement to reach the doormats of that countrywide horde of registrants, your local Job Centre can put you in touch with the nearest PER office.

I don't intend to teach you to suck eggs about other sources of recruitment, like commercial employment agencies, consultants and so on – but, rather, having mentioned advertisements, would now like you to sink your gnashers into the real meat of this chapter's sandwich.

All about recruitment sources and advertisements 37

EFFECTIVE RECRUITMENT ADVERTISING

THE AIMS

The manager who pours money into the bottomless pit of recruitment advertising without due regard for the aims of the process is, in short, a pound-spewing idiot. And, before we remind ourselves of these all-important objectives, I'm going to thump that one point home. . . . The aims are *not* something to be swiftly read and, equally swiftly, forgotten – *they should be borne in mind on each and every occasion when it's necessary to think about advertising a job vacancy.*

To be effective, any recruiting advertisement must:

(a) Obtain an appropriate response. In other words, it must attract the right audience.

(b) Provide a fully adequate description of the post, expressed in clear, concise and attractive terms.

(c) Achieve an overall presentation which enhances the company image. Ask yourself, how does the quality of your recruitment advertising compare with that of your *marketing* publicity?

(d) Be of the *right* size, and placed in the *right* position in the *right* publication at the *right* time.

OBTAINING AN APPROPRIATE RESPONSE

Consider, if you will, the following classified ad, culled from the columns of my local rag:

TRAINEE INTERVIEWERS
required

Young people interested in seeing different faces and working with people their own age

Ring Mr *****
Huntingdon ******
2 p.m.–5 p.m.

Did that abortion stand any chance of attracting the right audience? No way – unless, of course, the advertiser was a wily rascal who merely wished to tempt the unthinking dross to apply for what, in reality, was a horrible job of work. If, however, Mr 'X' really required young people suitable for training as interviewers – well, he stood a mighty poor chance of getting them.

Here is another example for your consideration.

One might be forgiven for thinking that any necessary technical qualifications and/or experience should have figured somewhere in the list of that advertiser's 'prime requirements' – which, let's face it, would have greatly increased his chances of obtaining an appropriate response.

PROVIDING A CLEAR, CONCISE AND ATTRACTIVE DESCRIPTION OF THE POST

Take a good look at this beauty.

> ## LADIES!
>
> Do you like driving, being out in the open air, are physically fit, aged between 20–35, have a clean driving licence and a talent for DIY and live within a 5-mile radius of Huntingdon?
>
> If the answer is yes, you are the lady we are looking for. We are a nationwide service company based in Huntingdon, looking for more staff to join our successful, ever-expanding company.
>
> *To find out more*
> Telephone Barbara on Huntingdon *******

What do you reckon – in this probable 'driving-type' job, does the reference to a 'talent for DIY' indicate that the successful applicants will be responsible for coping with their own roadside breakdowns, or does it imply that the work will involve dealing in some way with DIY products? And, since the advertiser mentions physical fitness, is it, just perhaps, the case that the lucky ladies will be required to tote half-tonne loads up and down garden paths, or what? What in hell *is* the job and, more to the point, where is there even a scrap of evidence that a job description was in existence – let alone used?

All of which constitutes an introduction to my next little item. . . .

THE SCRAN-BAG OF RECRUITMENT ADVERTISERS' FLANNEL

The manager who lacks faith in the quality of the post he is advertising, who wouldn't know an employee specification from Adam, who wishes nothing better than to pull the wool over the eyes of A. N. Other, or who is just plain dumb – this is the creature who resorts to the atrocious art of padding-out his ads with meaningless nonsense. Lest you doubt this, cast your peepers over just a few such horror-phrases.

> . . . we are looking for a caring person . . .
> . . . we offer excellent working conditions . . .
> . . . a forward-looking and progressive company . . .
> . . . an excellent rate of pay . . .
> . . . to join a lively and hard-working team . . .
> . . . our friendly, family-run business . . .
> . . . a challenging and rewarding position . . .
> . . . this prestigious and successful company . . .
> . . . the work is varied and interesting . . .
> . . . an exciting post . . . (!!)
> . . . an innovative and sophisticated organization . . .
> . . . an exciting, varied, sometimes hectic job . . .
> . . . a demanding and totally involving position . . .
> . . . this long-established and caring company . . .
> . . . totally committed to its employees . . .

To some it may be a hard pill to swallow, but it *is* possible to compose the text of any recruitment ad without resorting to these junk and, quite often, criminally fictional clichés. To back up my assertion, here are some examples.

All about recruitment sources and advertisements 41

MANAGEMENT AUDIT
with potential for career
development
£10,500–£12,750 + Car + Benefits

The Kopke Group, with a turnover of some £2,000 million in the last fiscal year, offers career opportunities in Management Audit.

We are seeking Accountants aged 22–27 years with good academic and professional qualifications to work within a small, London-based team. The management audits cover a programme of positive and constructive appraisals of Kopke organization, systems and trading activities. It is regarded in the Group as a management tool and not as an end in itself. The experience gained in this function will enhance promotion prospects in line management.

Candidates should be qualified accountants with an analytical approach to problems and the ability to express themselves clearly in written reports – and verbally, as they will be liaising with management at all levels and in all functions on a day-to-day basis. We offer highly competitive salaries with a company car and a full range of other benefits, including free BUPA membership, subsidized holidays and a non-contributory pension scheme. *Please apply in writing to Richard L. Hickory, Group Personnel Manager, Kopke PLC, Kopke House, 35–39 Anderson Street, London EC2Y 8DS*

KOPKE   The leaders in diagnostic equipment

ADMINISTRATIVE
ASSISTANT
Salary £10,450–£12,750 pa

An Assistant is required in our Conference Marketing Department to provide general secretarial and administrative services to the Conference Director. Applicants should be accustomed to working at senior level and should possess demonstrably superior shorthand and typing skills.

Hours 9 a.m.–5.15 p.m., 21 days' holiday, contributory pension scheme, interest-free loan facilities for annual season tickets.

Please apply in writing to G. H. Parsons, Conference Director, BK Consultants Ltd, 12 Devon Street, London WC2Y 4NV.

BK CONSULTANTS LIMITED

42 *The Secrets of Successful Hiring and Firing*

FARM WORKER REQUIRED
(Agricultural)

Minimum of 5 years' experience in all aspects of root crop production and the operation of modern farm machinery is essential. NUAAW rates of pay plus productivity bonus scheme. Three-bedroom, modern cottage accommodation is available.

Please apply to T. Atkins, Manor Farm, Cuttesley, Bude.

THE CROWN THEATRE, BIDEFORD

PUBLICITY MANAGER

Salary range £12,500–£14,250 pa

The Publicity Manager is responsible for ensuring that the positive image of the Crown Theatre is reflected and reinforced throughout all our publicity media from press advertising, posters and brochures through to the Annual Report. Close liaison with the Theatre's advertising agency and other outside professionals forms an essential part of the work. The Publicity Manager is also concerned with identifying opportunities and implementing detailed plans for the Theatre's future success.

Applicants should note that a minimum of five years' experience in publicity, marketing or a related discipline is essential.

Please apply for an application form to Susan Rutherford, The Crown Theatre, Bideford, North Devon EX44 5RX (Tel: 02 372 886123). The closing date for applications is 6 January 1988.

We are an equal opportunities employer

EDITORIAL ASSISTANT
Ashford, Kent

**Salary £8,500–£12,200
depending on allowances**

This is a new post. The successful applicant will have fast, accurate touch-typing ability and the willingness to grapple with new technology. The job entails sharing the running of a small office with one other person and taking on normal secretarial duties. Training in photo-typesetting will be provided and there will be the opportunity for occasional editorial and photo research.

Please write for an application form and full job description to George M. Hyde, General Manager, Zetland Magazines Ltd, Portal House, High Street, Ashford, Kent.

All about recruitment sources and advertisements **43**

If a job is worth advertising, it's certainly worth describing – and especially so if you wish to avoid receiving a stack of hopelessly unsuitable applications.

ENHANCING THE COMPANY IMAGE

There may be little opportunity to trumpet a company's image within the all-too-restricted confines of a tiny, classified ad – but the thinking manager will always ensure that his £2.50 for twenty words, or whatever, is spent wisely. A poorly worded advertisement (and the classified columns, in particular, are full of them) does very little for an employer's reputation, so think on it. Being beastly frank, if you're one of the legion of managers who has difficulty in slinging words together clearly, concisely and *effectively* – well, then, be honest with yourself and get someone else to write your ads.

When it comes to drafting the text and layout for a larger, display-type recruitment ad, take a crafty look at the pages and pages of them that appear in the national press, and learn from the professionals how to enhance your company image. Remember, also, that the price of inserting your ad normally includes some valuable free advice from the art department of the publication concerned – in other words, make them earn their money.

THE FOUR 'RIGHTS'

Choosing the right size of advertisement

All right, that wretched budget constraint usually reigns supreme, but the hard fact is, a couple of single column centimetres of classified space will not exactly set would-be applicants dancing in the streets – assuming, of course, that they spot the thing. If you've literally no choice but to air your recruiting needs in the classified columns, do ensure that you opt for a *semi-display* format – thereby gaining, at

44   *The Secrets of Successful Hiring and Firing*

the very least, suitably positioned headlines and a 'frame' in which to project your pearly words.

Choosing the right position
Apparently, or so the pundits tell us, when A. N. Other is scanning a page of recruiting ads, his or her peepers will fly straight to the top right-hand corner of said page – and it therefore follows that this is where your masterpiece should appear. Huh, easily said. . . . But hold on a tick, if you're planning to advertise in the local rag, it may well be that you *can* wield sufficient clout (but only if you are thinking in terms of a display-type ad) in order to bag this prime position. One thing is for certain, it is in matters such as this that, rather than indulge in the traditional telephone call, a personal visit to the paper's advertising department will prove a much better ploy.

If, once again, you're financially stuck with the classified columns, do check with the newspaper that your ad will appear under a relevant section heading; i.e., Clerical, Sales, etc. And, if there isn't a suitable heading, insist that one is provided, PDQ. . . . Believe me, the last thing you want is for your hopeful insertion to be consigned to that classified leper colony, the Miscellaneous section.

Choosing the right publication
While I'm sure you'd be inclined to think twice before advertising for a pig swill shoveller within the pages of the *Investors Chronicle*, there are some ground-rules to be borne in mind:

Professional/trade journals	These are ideal for the recruitment of executive and specialist personnel when *time* is not an essential factor. Plainly, while such periodicals enjoy limited circulations, their highly relevant readerships offer fertile picking-grounds for the aspiring recruiter.

National newspapers	You'll be more than familiar with the fact that the so-called 'quality press' attracts quality recruiting ads – and for very good reason, too. If you have the money (and, by George, it had better be a fair-sized Piggy Bank) and you're urgently seeking a whacking great audience, then go for the national newspapers.
Provincial newspapers	In addition to being the good old advertising standby for 'run-of-the-mill' vacancies, a provincial-type paper is often a useful vehicle for the advertisement of higher-grade slots – *provided* one gives more than a smidgin' of thought to the circulation and readership concerned. It's also worth re-membering that the traditional provincials are tending to lose a lot of readers (and, hence, a goodly number of recruiting ads) to their new-style, hefty com-petitors, the trader-type freebies – whose advertising rates, by the way, are generally cheaper.

Choosing the right time

I'm well aware that most vacancies are required to be filled yesterday – but, for goodness sake, don't let this prevent you scanning your chosen daily newspaper, especially if it's a national, in order to spot their 'peak' days for this or that type of vacancy. For instance, if it means that, on a particular day of the week, your extremely costly display ad for a master chef would almost certainly be swamped by a

46　The Secrets of Successful Hiring and Firing

welter of advertised sales and marketing vacancies – then, it is far better to bide your impatient time. And don't forget, unless you're in the market for a footballer or what-not, the average British job-seeker tends to hibernate on a Saturday.

THE NASTY BUSINESS OF 'BLINKERED' ADS

The employer who uses a box number in his recruiting ad has usually got something to hide, such as the fact that the hapless, present incumbent of a post doesn't even know that his scallywag boss is quietly seeking his replacement. Alternatively, a company may have such a bad name in the recruitment world that it is forced to advertise under this dubious shroud of anonymity. But, then, your firm would never dream of hiding its shining light under a box number bushel, would it?

In similar vein, the employer who resorts to those horrible words 'salary negotiable' deserves a fate worse than death. Such a miscreant is either a bazaar-type haggler over pay – or, more likely, just plain scared that, if he indicates an amount, his existing employees will see his ad and realize that *their* pay is way under that which is on offer.

Don't succumb to the use of blinkered advertisements – it's a dirty habit and it can send you blind.

AND, FINALLY, A SPOT OF HELP

Eyes down and looking for some hopeful aids to composition. . . .

A dial-an-ad phrase bank

Note: Add, change or delete words at will – always remembering that your aim is to fill your text with definitive information, not garbage.

. . . reporting to the . . . Director/Manager, the principal responsibilities will encompass . . .

All about recruitment sources and advertisements 47

. . . the successful applicant will be a qualified . . . preferably aged between . . . and . . .

. . . who is probably currently working in a . . . or . . . environment . . .

. . . you would be directly responsible to the . . . Director/Manager and be given total responsibility for the . . . aspects of . . . subsidiary companies . . .

. . . the successful applicant will head a multi-discipline team maintaining and installing . . . equipment at . . .

. . . the successful applicant, aged . . . to . . . , will have at least . . . years' experience in . . . , and be conversant with all aspects of . . .

. . . we require a . . . who will have gained several years' experience in the . . . industry in a . . . position . . .

. . . we are seeking a highly qualified . . . with experience in the . . . sector for development of . . . programmes on . . .

. . . reporting to the . . . , your ongoing brief will be to review . . . and to identify ways of making the whole operation more efficient . . .

. . . you will possess . . . and a sound . . . background, together with an eye for detail and the ability to organize . . .

. . . this is an influential role, reporting directly to the head of the . . . function, in which you will be responsible for the continued development and expansion of . . .

. . . applications are invited for the appointment of . . .

. . . the . . . department has vacancies for . . . with wide background experience in . . .

. . . in your mid- . . . s and almost certainly from a . . . background, your . . . years' experience will enable you to handle the . . .

. . . your role will be to fulfil the . . . activity as well as . . .

. . . aged at least . . . and with a broad based . . . background, you should have a minimum of . . . years' experience as a . . .

. . . we are currently seeking a highly qualified and experienced . . . , with a thorough knowledge of the . . . industry, to play a significant role in . . .

. . . qualified to . . . level in . . . , you should have at least . . . years' experience gained preferably in an . . . or . . . environment . . .

. . . you will be responsible for the . . . and the maintenance of the . . .

. . . the position is open to applicants with a proven record of physical fitness aged between . . . and . . . years . . .

. . . you will need . . . years' . . . experience in a professional commercial environment with a track record of successful application of company policies and procedures . . .

. . . combined with an adequate generalist background, you should have sound . . . experience and the ability to . . .

. . . our ideal candidate will be professionally qualified in an appropriate discipline; for example, ... You must have a minimum of . . . years' experience in a similar role, at least part of which will have given you sharp end exposure to . . .

. . . the salary will be £ . . . Other benefits include . . .

. . . salary £ . . . –£ . . . according to qualifications, experience and level of appointment . . .

. . . relocation assistance may be available . . .

. . . in addition to a salary of £ . . . , a generous relocation package will be offered where appropriate . . .

All about recruitment sources and advertisements 49

. . . the salary scale is reviewed annually and other
benefits include . . .

. . . in return for your considerable abilities, we
offer . . .

. . . this is a permanent position on a one-year renew-
able contract basis . . .

. . . ideally you should be resident, or prepared to
relocate with generous assistance, within a . . .
mile radius of . . .

. . . applicants of either sex please telephone for an
application form to . . .

. . . if you are interested in joining . . . , please
telephone for an application form to . . .

. . . alternatively, if you would like to discuss technical aspects of the work, or how your experience
may match our requirements, please call . . .

. . . the position, which will involve regular travel
within the UK and occasionally overseas,
offers . . .

. . . to find out more about this appointment, please
call . . .

In expressing the hope that your advertising seedlings will
bear peerless fruit, I'm bound to remind you that, in this
sceptred isle, if not in other countries, the law has something quite definite to say about our subject – so we'd better
round off this chapter with some legal-beagle stuff.

You'll probably be aware that it is unlawful discrimination to publish, or, as the law says, cause to be published,
any advertisement which indicates an intention to discrimi-
nate against members of a particular racial group, persons
of one sex or the other, or married persons – other than
when certain exclusions apply, as explained in the Codes of
Practice issued by the Equal Opportunities Commission
and the Commission for Racial Equality. Hence, for
example, the now popular and very wise phrase that
appears in so many recruiting ads:

WE ARE AN EQUAL OPPORTUNITIES EMPLOYER

We should also remember that the Sex Discrimination Act 1975 prohibits the use of job titles with a sexual or racial connotation – and lists 'waiter', 'salesgirl', 'postman' and 'stewardess' as handy examples of such transgressions. We all know the result of this chunk of law – a proliferation of fairly advertised jobs such as 'bar person', 'sales person' and the like.

In sum, to avoid discrimination your recruitment advertising should encourage applications from suitable candidates of all racial backgrounds and of both sexes. This not only means that ads must be carefully worded, but also that they must be placed in publications likely to be read by both sexes. Furthermore, one's advertising blurbs must refrain from presenting men and women in stereotyped roles – for example, it is unlawful to word an ad in such a crafty way that it would lead members of one sex or the other to believe that they would be unsuccessful in applying for the job concerned:

WANTED

BRICKLAYERS

Prospects for permanent employment. Good rates of pay. Applicants must be prepared to strip to the waist during summer. Apply to G. Bloggs, Huntingdon 597342

So now you know!

4 Short-listing and interview techniques

Come into my parlour, said the spider to the fly

Drop a hint to the average manager that there's some short-listing and interviewing to be done – and, in no time flat, he'll start thinking in terms of urgent family business in the Orkneys. There's a very good reason for this widespread antipathy – for, of all the tasks that Jack and Jill Executive are ill-equipped to face, the business of selecting people must surely take the cake. Lest you condemn this opener as a sweeping generalization, just consider – how many managers in your acquaintance have undergone formal training in picking the human wheat from the chaff? And, not to put too fine a point on it, have you been so lucky? The sad fact is, of all the executives who are authorized to select and hire employees, around 95 per cent have received no such training – and are forced (or choose) to get by on a dangerous amalgam of native wit and cunning.

Which is where we pause for the classic hail of comment. . . .

'Rubbish. . . . I may not like the task very much, but I've been in this game for over ten years – and, in that time, I've selected more employees than you've had hot dinners. . . .'

(One is tempted to ask this worthy if his massive engagement in selection has been necessitated by an equally massive labour turnover. . . .)

> 'Y'know, Goodworth, the trouble with blokes like you is, you're out of touch with reality. . . . Selection's been going on since the year dot and, no matter what gobbledegook you dream up, you can't alter the fact that a manager who knows his onions isn't likely to drop too many clangers.'

(If this broadside happens to reflect your sentiments, reader, one could pose the question, 'In that case, why in hell are you reading this book?' – but that would be very rude, so I won't.)

> 'There's always someone who's trying to have a dig at managers – and that's exactly what you're doing. . . . Look, off-hand, I don't know how many people I've selected for jobs, but it must be a fair old number – and, hey, I haven't been sacked yet. . . .'

(In response, a thought-jogger. . . . How many bosses, when faced with a significantly high proportion of resignations and dismissals, actually take the decision to overhaul their selection procedures – instead of merely falling on their backs and thinking of the Empire?)

Now that the flak has subsided, I'll put my steel helmet away – and, without further ado, invite you to accompany me on a look-see safari through the selection jungle.

CONTEMPLATING THE APPLICATION IN-TRAY

Having devoted a whole chapter to the subject of application forms, it's high time that we dealt with that other and alternative piece of candidate's paper, the *curriculum vitae*. You know, I'm more than convinced that any untrained selector should avoid the use of CVs like the plague – for, in my view, they spell nothing but trouble. To illustrate my point, I'd like you to imagine that you've harvested the fruits of a recruiting ad and, following your specific request for detailed CVs, you now have a mini-pile of them sitting in your in-tray. Let's riffle through these painfully composed personal histories and, in essence, see what we've got.

But, first, note the nondescript nature of the bunch, as a whole. Several have been handwritten on A5 Basildon Bond-type stationery, with one such effort actually running to five, paper-clipped pages of scrawl. Some have been fairly neatly typed on paper of varying shades and sizes – and the odd couple have been thoroughly mistyped on the worst of bank-weight paper. One applicant has presented his almost illegible handwriting on stuff that looks suspiciously like pages torn from a secretary's note-pad – and, look, tucked away at the bottom of the collection, there's a three-page *magnum opus* set out on foolscap. . . .

'All right, Clive – so what?'

Well, add to this the overriding factor that each one of these CVs has been compiled to individual whim, with bits and pieces of information (remember, some legible, some not) *recorded in a bewildering variety of formats*. In truth, our mini-pile represents nothing less than the selector's worst enemy – a thoroughly 'non-standard' clump of applications. All of which brings us face-to-face with the very next task.

THE SHORT-LISTING PROCESS

There is no magic formula for short-listing success – for, after all, its efficacy depends entirely on our very individual and wide-ranging abilities to extrapolate, interpret and weigh the information placed in front of us. However, there are a few tips:

56 *The Secrets of Successful Hiring and Firing*

1 As I've intimated, make the task that much easier by utilizing a well-designed, standardized application form. Then, at the very least, you will know *where* to look for specific items of information – and, hopefully, because it has been triggered by specific questions, it'll be the data you need.

2 Never attempt to short-list candidates without the use of a detailed employee specification:

   (a) A summary of the knowledge and skills required for the job.
   (b) Details of the education/technical/professional qualifications required.
   (c) The type and depth of experience sought.
   (d) Any necessary physical criteria.
   (e) Any special requirements; e.g., age, degree of mobility, etc.

   As I've intimated earlier, there are many wise-acre managers who tend to scoff and fall off their chairs laughing at the thought of even compiling, let alone using, employee specifications. Such over-confident know-alls usually profess with some asperity that any manager worth his or her salt will be more than familiar with what's required – that this piece of paper is yet another example of time-wasting bureaucracy. I'll content myself with a single comment: maintain such an attitude at your peril.

3 Do not be over-offended by what, in your view, is poor handwriting. Nowadays, very few jobs require Dickensian standards of copperplate – and, anyway, what's *your* handwriting like, eh?

4 Remember that you're seeking someone with all-round fire in the belly, and pay a goodly amount of attention to stated hobbies and leisure pursuits. It's a fair assumption that the applicant who provides a fulsome description of spare-time interests (as opposed to an uninformative

list) is an individual who doesn't switch off at the drop of a hat.

5 When endeavouring to interpret and weigh applicants' information, keep a constant lookout for probable embroidery (and, of course, potential downright lies), but do not be inclined to condemn at the short-listing stage – you could be wrong.

A DIG ON RUDENESS AND CRUELTY PERSONIFIED

The employer who completes his short-listing process and then ditches the rejected applications *without so much as an acknowledgement* is a discourteous and heartless creature who, for my money, should be shot on sight. There is nothing quite so sickening or demotivating to a person who is striving to land a job than to have an application treated with such arrant disregard. I'll make no bones about this one – if you're such an employer (and I sincerely trust you are not), then pull your finger out and, for the price of a stamp and some typing, conduct your selection affairs with a grain of common decency:

Dear Mr Brown

Thank you for your application for the post of Office Supervisor within this company.

Sadly, I must inform you that, despite the most careful consideration, we are unable to take your application further on this occasion.

I do hope that this will not be too much of a disappointment, and would like to wish you every success in your search for suitable employment.

Yours sincerely

PREPARING FOR THE FRAY

An employment interview is, or jolly well should be a *friendly, steered discussion*, conducted with the primary aim of seeking out and verifying the facts of an applicant's past successes and failures. Note the term 'friendly' and, if you are wise, always bend over backwards to extend this amicable approach to every facet of your selection process – including the invitation to interview:

Dear Miss Spencer

Thank you for your most interesting application for the post of Credit Control Clerk within this company.

Having studied this in some depth, I would like to take things a stage further – and, to this end, would ask that you kindly attend for interview at this office on 16 August at 10.00 a.m. Perhaps you would be good enough to confirm the appointment by ringing my secretary, Miss Luke, as soon as possible.

I look forward to meeting you in person.

Yours sincerely

So, we've now reached the point where selected applicants will be feverishly donning their best bibs and tuckers (well, at any rate, some of them) and turning up for interview. But, before we get to grips with that dreaded bit, there's a question to be posed – namely, how are these bright-eyed and bushy-tailed candidates going to fare on arrival at your premises? Consider the following checklist, and see how *your* outfit makes out when it comes to the reception and general treatment of interviewees.

A CHECKLIST ON THE INTERVIEW ENVIRONMENT

1   When arranging your interview schedule, do you allow at least twenty minutes after each session for the all-important business of post-interview assessment? The selector who leaves this task until all the candidates have been seen is simply asking for trouble.

2   When allocating appointment times, do you make full allowance for any candidates who will be coming from some distance away?

3   Have a deep think about this one – what is that little girl in reception *really* like at her job? Are you truly confident that candidates will be received pleasantly and efficiently – or is your outfit one of the many where the vital job of reception is plonked on a telephonist-cum-typist's shoulders as an unconsidered afterthought?

4   And what of the reception area, itself? Is it decently appointed – or, in truth, does it more closely resemble the kind of place Silas Marner would have favoured? Does a dog-eared, year-old copy of some trade journal or other really constitute attractive reading matter?

5   Do you always ensure that whoever wheels the candidates into your presence performs this small but important task with bright and breezy aplomb? And does he or she always remind each candidate of your name?

6   If you reimburse candidates' travelling expenses (and you damned well should do), are you happy that this is done briskly and efficiently? Like, for instance, ensuring that the receptionist oversees the completion of claim forms or whatever, while your secretary doles out the cash?

7   And what about that holy of holies, the interview room? Immediately prior to the sessions, do you check that:
(a)   The place is clean and tidy?

60 *The Secrets of Successful Hiring and Firing*

   (b)   The interview hot-seat is adequately comfortable and positioned in such a way that the sun will not be blazing directly into the candidates' eyes?

   (c)   The telephone is cut off?

   (d)   If unprotected by a secretary, your 'Interview in progress – do not disturb' sign is in place?

   (e)   Extraneous noise is reduced to a minimum?

Let me round off this section by stating and emphasizing the obvious. . . . The overall environment in which interviews are conducted will have a profound effect on their outcome – and, if you want your candidates to give of their best, you know what you have to do, don't you?

And now, there's no option, we've got to chew on the tough old meat in the selection sandwich – the interview, itself.

WATCH OUT, I'M SHOVING YOU IN AT THE DEEP END

What are you like as an interviewer? No, don't tell me, tell yourself – and, as a crafty kick along the road to introspective home-truths, here is a somewhat lengthy questionnaire for you to tackle. Be a devil, have a go – and make a note of your responses. You'll need to refer to them later on.

A QUESTIONNAIRE ON INTERVIEWING SKILLS AND APTITUDES

Self-candour is the secret – and, remember, since you have no witnesses, you *can* afford to indulge in the truth.

1   Do you *dislike* the task of interviewing applicants for employment?

   (a)   Not at all – in fact, I enjoy it.   . . . . .

   (b)   Well, slightly – put it this way, I'd rather be

Short-listing and interview techniques 61

     doing something else.   . . . . .
(c)   Yes, I find it quite unpleasant.   . . . . .
(d)   'Dislike' is an understatement – I detest interviewing strangers.   . . . . .

2 More to the point, do you *worry* about your overall performance as an employment interviewer?
(a)   No – this has never caused me any anxiety.. . . .
(b)   Yes, to the extent that I often wonder if my performance is really up to scratch.   . . . . .
(c)   Yes, the mere thought of conducting an employment interview causes me a great deal of anxiety.   . . . . .

3 What about the opening phase of such an interview – the business of breaking the ice? Do you:
(a)   Experience no trouble at all in kicking off from square one?   . . . . .
(b)   Sometimes feel that your efforts at conversation tend to be trite or even banal?   . . . . .
(c)   Experience great difficulty in surmounting this initial hurdle?   . . . . .

4 When conducting an employment interview, do you:
(a)   Rely on the candidate's application form as a guide for your questioning; i.e., systematically 'go through it' from beginning to end, posing questions where necessary?   . . . . .
(b)   Follow some other, predetermined interview plan?   . . . . .
(c)   Follow no such definite plan, in that (although you obviously refer to the application form) you prefer the interview to be a 'free-ranging' session?   . . . . .

5 While the majority of interview questions should be devoted to establishing the facts of an applicant's past experience and background, some should aim at placing the candidate on his mettle – by testing his ability to sell himself, cope with criticism and so on.

62   *The Secrets of Successful Hiring and Firing*

Which of the following responses most closely matches your reaction to the above statement?

(a) I fully agree. Replies to such questions provide the interviewer with valuable clues concerning the applicant's strengths and weaknesses of character. . . . . .

(b) I see no harm in such questions – and, anyway, candidates expect to be asked them. . . . .

(c) I disagree – I think such questions are unfair to the candidate. . . . . .

(d) I disagree – I think such questions are simply a waste of time. . . . .

6 Be beastly frank with yourself – do your nearest and dearest ever accuse you of interrupting them in mid-sentence? Are you a person who tends to 'break in' when other people are speaking – albeit due to enthusiasm, or because what they are saying is wrong?

(a) Guilty as charged, me lud. . . . . .

(b) Well, just occasionally. . . . . .

(c) Practically never – I'm a very good listener.. . . .

7 Again, very frankly, would you say that you are blessed with powers of 'natural leadership'?

(a) Yes, most certainly – I know this to be true.. . . .

(b) Let's put it this way. . . . I seldom, if ever, have any trouble in making my views known to others – if that's what you mean. While I may not be the world's best leader, I'm no shrinking violet. . . . .

(c) No, I don't *think* so. . . . . .

(d) My God, no – I'm the very reverse. . . . .

8 Do you suffer fools gladly?

(a) No, I don't – especially when they ask such damn-fool questions. . . . .

(b) I try to be patient, but must admit that I don't always succeed. , ...

Short-listing and interview techniques 63

(c) Of course I do – after all, they're part and parcel of life's rich tapestry, aren't they? . . . . .

9 Do you take pleasure in advising and helping people with their problems?

(a) Yes, I do – and if more people did the same, the world would be a better place. . . . . .

(b) On occasion – and especially when I am asked. . . . . .

(c) I won't refuse anyone who asks for my help or advice, but I certainly don't go out of my way to volunteer it – there are far too many busy-bodies around, as it is. . . . . .

10 Have your nearest and dearest ever told you that you're an argumentative so-and-so? *Do* you like to argue the point with people – albeit in a pleasant manner?

(a) Yes, I'll say! . . . . .

(b) I only engage in argument when the occasion demands. . . . . .

(c) I dislike argument and do my best to avoid it. . . . . .

11 Sadly, it's often the case that a manager's performance in his job is inhibited by the policies imposed on him and/or the attitudes of his seniors. In this context, which of the following most closely approximates to *your* point of view?

(a) I have absolutely no such worries. In fact, it's a constant source of satisfaction to me that I'm lucky enough to work within a framework of good, sound policies imposed and implemented by a first-rate management. . . . . .

(b) Look, there's no such thing as a perfect working environment, but I reckon I'm luckier than most. . . . Of course, there are times when I get niggled and even frustrated by some aspect of policy or attitude of 'them

64   *The Secrets of Successful Hiring and Firing*

      upstairs' – but, hell, who doesn't?   . . . . .

(c)   Y'know, you're dead right. . . . There are many ways in which my job would be easier *and* more enjoyable if only the policies were realistic – to say nothing of the attitudes of some of those at the top.   . . . . .

(d)   So far as I'm concerned, that's the under-statement of the century. . . . I have the misfortune to work for a firm that's up to the gunnels in ridiculous policies – which are matched only in idiocy by the bunch of cretins who implement them.   . . . . .

12   Are you a manager who 'has come up the hard way'?

(a)   Yes, I certainly am – and I'm proud of it . . . . .

(b)   I never think of my career in such terms – but I haven't always been a manager, if that's what you mean.   . . . . .

(c)   No, I'm not.   . . . . .

13   If you believe in common with most managers that a job applicant's personality must be taken into consideration at interview, exactly how do *you* go about assessing this factor?

(a)   Well, firstly, I don't go in for any deliberate attempts to assess personality – after all, I'm not a psychologist. . . . Let me put it this way – normally, by the end of an interview session, I've seen and heard enough to enable me to form a pretty fair impression of what makes the candidate tick.   . . . . .

(b)   Oh, that's a simple one to answer. I bend over backwards to encourage the candidate to talk – mainly, by seeking his views on this or that topical subject. This way, things like maturity, leadership qualities and what-not start to peep through. . . .   .

(c)   It goes without saying, doesn't it, that

Short-listing and interview techniques 65

nearly all candidates 'put on an act' at interview – and I think it's essential that one peels away this false veneer. In my view, this is best done by posing questions that, well, jog them out of their complacency. The stickier the questions, the better. . . . That's how I get at the truth, personality-wise. . . . .

14 Have you undergone any formal training in employment interviewing?

(a) Yes. I've completed a full-time course of five or more days' duration. . . . . .

(b) Yes. I've completed a full-time course of one to four days' duration. . . . . .

(c) Yes – I once attended a half-day course in employment interviewing. . . . . .

(d) No – but I have taken the trouble to read up on the subject. . . . . .

(e) No – but I have been interviewing for quite some time. It's true to say that I've picked up quite a few wrinkles since my initial stabs at the game. . . . .

(f) No – and, despite whatever experience I've gained, I feel I should undergo some sort of formal training. . . . . .

15 Finally, how do you rate yourself as an employment interviewer?

(a) I consider myself to be first-rate. . . . . .

(b) Quite proficient, I guess. . . . . .

(c) If I'm honest, not too good. . . . . .

(d) I'm a terrible interviewer. . . . . .

Well, there we have it, a thoroughly non-scientific questionnaire – designed with the sole intention of encouraging you to take a long, hard look at your interviewing warts. And now, as if you didn't know, we come to the indigestible bit. I'd like you to consider your fifteen

66 The Secrets of Successful Hiring and Firing

responses in the light of the following comments – and, before you start, it's probably worth repeating that utter self-candour is the name of the game.

1 Do you *dislike* the task of interviewing applicants for employment?

Response (a) Genuine enjoyment of the interviewing task is one, highly commendable thing, but enjoyment derived at the candidate's expense is quite another. So, ask yourself, *why* do you enjoy it? Is it, perhaps, that the business of sitting in judgement over hapless applicants for employment makes you feel good inside? Do you, in fact, regard the interview as a heaven-sent opportunity to act the big wheel in front of a captive audience? If you are guilty of taking such ego trips, you can be quite certain that your overall interviewing style will reflect your vanity – and, more to the point, that this arrant brand of egotism will tumble you headlong into making some pretty disastrous selection decisions.

Response (b) If you chose this response – why, welcome to the club! Research confirms that most averagely-effective interviewers gain only slight enjoyment from the task and, in general, would prefer to earn their daily bread doing something else.

Response (c) The manager who finds employment interviewing palpably unpleasant (as opposed to well-nigh unbearable) may well be suffering one of the penalties of soldiering on without the untold benefits of training in the technique. Since even the problem of innate shyness can be ameliorated by a dose of good training, is this not food for thought?

Response (d) If you, reader, honestly *detest* the interviewing task, then, whatever the circumstances, there is but one question to be posed – why in hell are you subjecting yourself, your unfortunate candidates

Short-listing and interview techniques 67

and your firm's selection process to such ruination? It is, of course, just possible that some first-class training would provide a solution to your problem – but if it doesn't (or hasn't), then *stop interviewing.*

2 More to the point, do you *worry* about your overall performance as an employment interviewer?

Response (a) The interviewer who suffers not the slightest anxiety over his performance stands in exactly the same danger as the actor who doesn't feel pre-curtain butterflies – in short, an inescapable date with Nemesis. So, if you responded thus, take my word for it, you're suffering from a nastily fatal dose of over-confidence.

Response (b) Good-oh, but remember, your oft-anxious thoughts will get you nowhere unless you pinpoint the root causes of your worry – and do something about them. Read on and, having read, make the decision to undergo whatever training is necessary.

Response (c) As in 1(d), above, there is no cosy answer. If your deep-seated and desperate anxiety cannot be cured by training, your course is clear – get out of the interviewing kitchen before the wretched heat burns you *and* your candidates to a frazzle.

3 What about the opening phase of such an interview – the business of breaking the ice? Do you:

Response (a) If, indeed, you experience no trouble at all in settling candidates down and thus getting your interviews off to a flying start, then good for you. But, er, dare I ask – would your interviewees agree with this rosy self-assessment?

Responses (b) and (c) Take heart, particularly if this is your only problem, for we're going to deal with the question of how best to break the interview ice a bit later on. In the meantime, use your introspection to good advantage and try to determine exactly *why* you

68   *The Secrets of Successful Hiring and Firing*

find this aspect of the interview a hard nut to crack.

4   When conducting an employment interview, do you:

Response (a)   While the application form provides an obvious and necessary 'base reference' for the conduct of any employment interview, it can constitute a nasty trap for the unwary. The interviewer who systematically 'goes through the thing' from beginning to end may succumb to the habit of overindulging in highly unprofitable direct questions; for example:

Q   'I see you gained five GCE 'O' levels. . . .'
A   'Yes.'
Q   'Fine. . . . Ah, yes, and your best grade is in English Language – did you enjoy English?'
A   'Yes, very much.'
Q   'Uh-huh. . . . Now, I see there's no mention of a pass in maths – this is obviously one of your weaker subjects. . . .'
A   'Yes, I'm afraid so. . . .'
Q   'Um. . . . Well, moving on, you mention that you were a house prefect – was this by election?'
A   'Er, no.'
Q   'Ah, you were appointed by the house master?'
A   'Yes, that's right.'
Q   'Well, it's still very much to your credit. . . . Now, what about this membership of the debating society – did you take an active part in the debates?'
A   'Yes, I quite enjoyed some of them.'
Q   'You like public speaking, then?'
A   'Er, yes – I quite like it.'

While the habit of posing direct questions (of which more anon) is a general interviewing malaise, there is no doubt that slavish adherence to the application form can trigger them off in vast quantities. Think on it and, teaching you to suck eggs, ask yourself – why are

Short-listing and interview techniques 69

direct questions so unprofitable?

Response (b) If you habitually follow some other, predetermined interview plan – good-oh. We'll be having a look at one or two such plans later in this chapter.

Response (c) If you opted for this response and you do, indeed, conduct your interviews without recourse to any plan, however simple – well, my friend, you've just qualified for the proverbial doghouse. I don't care if you do regard yourself as the best thing since sliced bread where mental acuity is concerned – you're a knave. I'll be having a further go at you later on.

5 While the majority of interview questions should be devoted to establishing the facts of an applicant's past experience and background, some should aim at placing the candidate on his mettle – by testing his ability to sell himself, cope with criticism and so on.

Which of the following responses most closely matches your reaction to the above statement:

Response (a) If you are engaged in the selection of applicants for sales and such-like jobs, it's more than likely that you will be much in favour of the 'stress interview' approach – because, as you'll probably tell me, you're in the market for people with that good old fire in the belly. All right, but when it comes to assessing these 'valuable clues concerning the applicant's strengths and weaknesses of character', there is a hard truth to be faced – very few interviewers are qualified for the task. Like it or not, such assessments of the candidate are filtered through the enormously subjective screen of the interviewer's own views and prejudices – and it takes a better man than you or I, Gunga Din, to escape this oft-alarming subjectivity of judgement.

Response (b) In (a), above, I've explained that the harm of such questions is enshrined in the wretchedly fallible brain-box of the interviewer – it's what he or

70 The Secrets of Successful Hiring and Firing

she makes of candidates' replies that is invariably harmful. As for interviewees expecting to be asked these $64,000 block-busters – well, that's absolutely no excuse for perpetrating the evil. Once again, more anon.

Responses (c) and (d) Right on both counts – although I believe that (c) really gets to the heart of the matter.

6 . . . do your nearest and dearest ever accuse you of interrupting them in mid-sentence? Are you a person who tends to 'break in' when other people are speaking – albeit due to enthusiasm, or because what they are saying is wrong?

Response (a) You should know what's coming. . . . The odds are that you constantly interrupt the poor old interview candidate, too – and that is reprehensible. No, don't interrupt me, just stop it.

Response (b) Just occasionally – *are you sure?*

Response (c) Well, I'll believe you, but would your long-suffering candidates agree, eh?

7 Again, very frankly (!), would you say that you are blessed with powers of 'natural leadership'?

Response (a) Stand by for a nasty dig in the ribs. . . . If you are so convinced that you enjoy powers of natural leadership, it's on the cards that you regularly set out to impress others (wilfully or involuntarily) with your convictions. So, are your interview candidates forced to endure gale-force demonstrations of your attributes as a born *Duce* among men? If so, I pity them.

Responses (b) and (c) Both are 'happy-average' responses – and, in either case, you're off the comment-hook.

Response (d) If you chose this alternative, it's almost certain that you dislike the interviewing task, and worry about it – so it's back to the comments of Questions 1 and 2 for you, chum.

Short-listing and interview techniques 71

8 Do you suffer fools gladly?

Response (a) A candidate deserves and has the right to expect the utmost in civility, tact and patience from his interviewer. Could it be that, in responding thus, you really should admit to some personal shortcomings where these vital requirements are concerned?

Response (b) Provided this *is* a nicely frank, middle-of-the-road response, I've no further comment.

Response (c) Marvellous. If you're being utterly truthful, you must have the patience of Job.

9 Do you take pleasure in advising and helping people with their problems?

Response (a) While it is admirable for one to take a distinct pleasure in assisting others with their problems, it is also a fact that people who are gifted with this attribute often make poor interviewers – in that an undue proportion of valuable interview time is devoted to the cause of helping and advising candidates, rather than *selecting* them. How say you?

Responses (b) and (c) So far as employment interviewing is concerned – no comment.

10 Have your nearest and dearest ever told you that you're an argumentative so-and-so? *Do* you like to argue the point with people – albeit in a pleasant manner?

Response (a) In addition to acknowledging that you're definitely an argumentative type, you must also acknowledge that this particular breed of leopard doesn't change his spots – whether you realize it or not, you're bound to be an *argumentative interviewer*. And, however much you may like putting your oar in, it's a heinous selection crime. No, don't argue – just take my word for it. . . .

Response (b) All okay – no comment.

Response (c) Hey, if you dislike argument and do

72 The Secrets of Successful Hiring and Firing

your best to avoid it, is this but one manifestation of your make-up as a wee timorous beastie of an interviewer? Well, only you can answer that one.

11   Sadly, it's often the case that a manager's performance in his job is inhibited by the policies imposed on him and/or the attitudes of his seniors. In this context, which of the following most closely approximates to *your* point of view?

Response (a)   Crikey, I envy you, you're one in a million – unless, that is, your name is Uriah Heep.

Responses (b) and (c)   As you well know, both of these responses echo the thoughts of managers the world over. As it was in the beginning, is now, and ever shall be. . . .

Response (d)   If, for real *or* imagined reasons, you have elected for this chilling response, the chances are that your deep-seated contempt for your organization will certainly be revealed, intentionally or unwittingly, to your interview candidates. While you may deem yourself fully entitled to feel disloyalty towards your firm, you have absolutely no right to infect applicants for employment with the bug. Enough said.

12   Are you a manager who 'has come up the hard way'?

Response (a)   The danger here is that many managers who are convinced that they've clawed their way up the ladder despite almost overwhelming odds *cannot help reminding other people of the fact.* I've heard them, and you've heard them; the point is, are you one such trumpeter – especially when it comes to that eyeball-to-eyeball confrontation with an interview candidate?

Response (b)   So, in responding thus, it's highly unlikely that you commit the sin noted in (a), above – which can only be good.

Response (c)   No comment, because I'm sure you don't prate to others (especially interview candidates)

Short-listing and interview techniques 73

about the swiftness of your accession to management –
do you?

13 If you believe in common with most managers that a
job applicant's personality must be taken into consideration at interview, exactly how do *you* go about
assessing this factor?

Response (a) It's probably fair to say that this is Mr
Average-Manager's response. In order that we can get
this business of assessing personality into some form of
perspective, I'd like you to read the comments for
responses (b) and (c), below.

Responses (b) and (c) These responses really only
vary in terms of interview tactics – one reflects the
softly-softly approach, while the other echoes the
philosophy of a manager who firmly believes in a
goodly dollop of stress interviewing – and, where the
latter is concerned, we're back to the sum and
substance of Question 5. The important thing is, in
addition to being ill-equipped to assess candidates'
replies to $64,000 questions, *we are desperately ill-
equipped when it comes to assessing personality.*

Lest you doubt this (and you may well do so, for
we're all infected to some extent with the 'I know a
good chap when I see one' syndrome), pause and
think. . . . If we were as good at assessing personality
as we often imagine; why, there would be no broken
marriages or friendships, no disagreement between
people, no such thing as war – and no selection
clangers.

The tragedy is, we need to engage in this examination of personality – so the message must be:

(i) Unless you are qualified and experienced in
psychological selection methods, *never* indulge in
personally-devised party tricks – like trying to
stump the candidate with awkward questions and
so on. If you must have near-definitive assess-

74 *The Secrets of Successful Hiring and Firing*

ments of personality, then make use of the well-validated personality tests and inventories which are available for exactly this purpose.

(ii)   Always remember that your personal assessment of a candidate can only be the product of an intensely subjective mental process – which, when you think about it, may be a very good reason for subjecting candidates to more than one interviewer. . . .

14   Have you undergone any formal training in employment interviewing?

Responses (a) and (b)   Terrific – and congratulations are in order, for you are members of the 4 to 5 per cent elite of managers who have been thus trained. However, if you elected for (b), when are you going to tackle a really worthwhile interviewing course?

Responses (c) and (d)   Totally inadequate. Get thee to a nunnery – and a decent interviewing course.

Response (e)   Aha, the manager who has been interviewing for five years is more than likely the guy or gal who picked up bad habits in the first year – and has perpetuated them ever since. For goodness sake, stop being so beastly sanguine – and get yourself trained.

Response (f)   So what are you waiting for, eh?

15   Finally, how do you rate yourself as an employment interviewer?

Response (a)   Gosh. . . . Why on earth are you reading this book?

Response (b)   Bully for you – so long as you are right.

Response (c)   And, being honest, what are you going to do about those weaknesses – other than continue to subject your poor old candidates to them?

Response (d)   Let's be deadly serious. . . . If you are such a rankly poor interviewer, you simply must be

Short-listing and interview techniques   75

fair to yourself and, come what may, *give it up*.

Well, I venture to suggest that if those questions haven't succeeded in provoking you to think about the manner in which you conduct interviews, nothing will. It's time we got on.

PLANNING THE INTERVIEW

Unless one is blessed with superfine grey matter between the ears, the practice of conducting unplanned, free-ranging interviews can be little short of disastrous – but that does *not* mean to say that we have to stick like glue to one or other of the well-known, published schemes. While these have considerable merit (we'll deal with a couple in a jiffy), particularly where the inexperienced interviewer is concerned, there is a simple, yet effective, alternative – and here it is.

The chronological approach
In a nutshell and although it sounds far too trite for words, select a convenient chronological point in the candidate's history – *and work steadily from this point through to the present day*. Because you are human, the interview will be peppered with side-issues and other hiccups – but, provided you always remember to steer the thing back to the chronological mainstream, you won't go far wrong.

In the event, however, that you favour a more structured plan, here are two widely known and proven schemes for your digestion.

The seven-point interview plan
(Professor Alec Rodger)

1   *Physical make-up.*   Health, bearing, overall appearance, quality of speech.

2 *Attainments.* Education, professional and/or technical qualifications, experience.
3 *General intelligence.* The candidate's basic intellectual ability.
4 *Specific aptitudes.* Special skills required – mechanical dexterity, manual dexterity, verbal/written communication, etc.
5 *Interests.* Intellectual, social, practical, physically active, etc.
6 *Disposition* (careful!). Aspects of maturity, reliability, leadership qualities, etc.
7 *Circumstances.* Domestic, degree of mobility, availability for irregular hours, etc.

The five-fold grading scheme
(J. Munro Fraser)

1 *Impact on others.* Relations with juniors, peers and colleagues. Physical make-up, manner, appearance, speech.
2 *Qualifications.* Education, professional and/or technical attainments, experience.
3 *Innate abilities.* Intelligence, alertness, aptitude for learning, etc.
4 *Motivation* (again, careful!). Enthusiasm, drive, quality of the goals set by the individual, etc.
5 *Adjustment* (beware of the minefield . . .). Emotional stability, ability to cope with stress and the unexpected, ability to integrate with groups, etc.

If there is a golden rule for planning an employment interview, it must be that the overall objective is to identify and examine the facts of a candidate's past achievements – for these are the only reliable predictors of future performance.

Short-listing and interview techniques 77

THE TECHNIQUE OF ASKING QUESTIONS IN THE RIGHT WAY

The interviewer who wishes to end up with bags of information *additional to that already contained within a candidate's application* will concentrate all his efforts on posing open-ended questions. And the best way to achieve this happy end is to remember and constantly resort to the 'magic six':

What   *What* were your primary responsibilities . . . ?
What made you decide . . . ?
What did you do then . . . ?
What courses did you take . . . ?
What other subjects did you . . . ?
What do you think of . . . ?
etc.

Why   *Why* did you decide to . . . ?
Why was that . . . ?
Why did you opt for . . . ?
Why did you leave . . . ?
Why did your firm . . . ?
Why did you choose . . . ?
etc.

When   *When* did that happen . . . ?
When did you first realize . . . ?
When was that . . . ?
When did your firm . . . ?
When did that come about . . . ?
When did you join . . . ?
etc.

Which   *Which* seemed best . . . ?
Which were your weakest . . . ?
Which was that . . . ?
Which did you really enjoy . . . ?
Which of these . . . ?

78 *The Secrets of Successful Hiring and Firing*

	Which course was that . . . ?
	etc.
Where	*Where* did you . . . ?
	Where was that . . . ?
	Where did they . . . ?
	Where is that . . . ?
	Where do you think . . . ?
	Where were you when . . . ?
	etc.
How	*How* did you go about this . . . ?
	How was that . . . ?
	How was your section organized . . . ?
	How did that come about . . . ?
	How did you manage to . . . ?
	How much assistance did you have . . . ?
	etc.

If you tackled the comments on the questionnaire (and I certainly hope you did), you'll recall that I've already made mention of two, nastily endemic interviewing weaknesses; namely, habitual use of direct questions and lip-smacking resort to those dubious beasties, $64,000 questions. The wise interviewer will remember the ground-rules.

Direct questions
Those that produce 'yes', 'no' or similarly unrewarding replies should only be used when absolutely necessary; for example:

● When 'settling-in' a candidate ('Did you have a decent journey here?' and so on).
● When it is required to confirm specific details ('Let me make certain that I've got this right – you joined ABC as a management trainee?' etc.).

$64,000 questions
The interviewer who doesn't regularly pose his pet version

Short-listing and interview techniques 79

of the classic terrifier, 'Tell me, why do you want this job?' is a rare creature, indeed. The big trouble is, we all have our intensely personal and, even with the best of us, prejudice-tainted conceptions of the 'right' answer – and, believe me, they vary like the March winds. We may not like it, but we simply have to accept the fact that – while a candidate's response may provide an *indication* of his powers of communication, maturity of thought and what-not – our judgement in such matters is dangerously subjective.

So, ask $64,000 questions if you must – *but handle them like eggs.*

Unfortunately, there is a further pitfall to be avoided in this business of asking questions the right way. . . .

Standard-revealing questions

These are questions which are phrased in such a manner that they betray the interviewer's own thoughts and/or company policy on the subject; for example:

Question	'Now, John, if there's one thing I can't stand, it's youngsters who have no interest in useful hobbies – so, tell me, what do *you* do in your spare time?'
Likely answer	'Oh, er, I enjoy drawing, sir, and – yes, I like modelling. And, er, there's helping old people – yes, I like doing that. . . .'
Question	'And what about those wretched, noisy discos, eh?'
Likely answer	'Oh, no – I don't have much time for that kind of thing. . . .'
Question	'Now, you do understand, Mr Giles, the successful applicant for this post will be a key member of our negotiating team – how do you see yourself coping in this respect?'
Likely answer	'Oh, let me assure you, I've absolutely no fears on that score, Mr Bloggs. . . . I much

80 *The Secrets of Successful Hiring and Firing*

enjoy this kind of cut-and-thrust activity – and, although I say it myself, negotiating's always been one of my stronger points. . . .'

All right, reader, I'm quite sure that you'd never think of using such a blatant approach – but, forgive me, is it just possible that you employ standard-revealing questions *without* thinking?

I reckon there's no better way of rounding of this section than to take a look at a number of worthwhile interview questions – remembering that, with the exception of those which are purely devoted to 'settling-in' the candidate, the interviewer's overall objective must be to achieve – yes, you've got it in one – a friendly, steered discussion; conducted with the primary aim of seeking out and verifying past successes and failures.

AN INTERVIEW SAMPLER

The vital 'settling-in' phase

'How do you do, Mr White – welcome to Appleyard Industries. I'm Brian Forbes, the personnel manager. . . . Do take a seat. . . . Did you have a decent journey here?'

'Good morning, young George. . . .' (*Reassuring smile*) 'It's nice to see you – I'm Brian Forbes, the company personnel manager. Do sit down and make yourself comfortable. . . . Did you come by bus or do you have your own transport?'

'Ah, you came by car. . . . What was the ring road like – the traffic's usually terrible at this time of day. . . .'

'Yes, I know what you mean – it makes one wonder what the so-called planners are up to. . . . Incidentally, I hope you were looked after in reception – did you get a cup of coffee?'

'Ah, you have a motorbike – I tell you, it's a long time since *I* had that pleasure. . . . What make is it?'

'Fine. . . . Well, now, I've had a good look at your application – and, plainly, I'm keen to find out some more about your most interesting background. . . . So, if you're comfortable, let's get cracking, shall we? What. . . .'

'Good. Well, now, having studied your application in some depth, I'd like to take things a stage further – and find out some more about your background. So, if you're seated comfortably, shall we make a start? What. . . .'

Probing a young candidate's schooling

'I see – that's most interesting. . . . Let's talk about things in general at Radcliffe – for instance, how was discipline implemented at the school?'

'Ah, yes, and I see from your application that you were a prefect. Tell me, how did this come about?'

'Uh-huh – and, as a prefect, what kind of powers did you have?'

'Well, I'm sure you used them wisely. . . . And what about extra-curricular activities – student groups, societies, and the like? I imagine there were quite a few – tell me something about them.'

'I see – and which of these did you join?'

'Did you, indeed! How did that come about?'

'Good. . . . Tell you what, let's turn to the dreaded, daily grind. . . . What was your favourite subject?'

'Why was that, do you think?'

'That's interesting. . . . What about the other side of the coin – what was your least favourite subject?'

'Ah, I wasn't too keen on that, myself! Why did you find it a bit of a drag?'

'I see. . . . Now, you've listed the grades you obtained in the 'O' levels, but I see no mention of mathematics – what happened here?'

82 *The Secrets of Successful Hiring and Firing*

'What do *you* think was the main reason for this?'

'And, tell me – if asked, what do you imagine your teacher would have to say about this?'

'Well, that's nicely frank! Changing the subject, how was the business of careers advice organized at Radcliffe?'

'And how did the careers advice master help you, personally?'

'Fair enough. . . . Tell me, George, how do you think things could have been improved?'

'So when did you first start thinking about a career in local government?'

'And how did that come about?'

Probing a candidate's employment

'Before we turn to the question of what you did at Fisher's, Mr Simpson, tell me a little about the company, in general. . . .'

'Fine. . . . What about your direct boss – what was his job title?'

'What were his main responsibilities?'

'And where did you fit into this picture?'

'I see. . . . Now, you've provided a brief description of your main duties in your application – perhaps you'd like to enlarge on this. . . .'

'Yes, most interesting. . . . Tell me, how many people were within your span of control – that's to say, reporting directly to you?'

'And, speaking of control, how much autonomy did you enjoy where the management of your team was concerned?'

'I understand. . . . In this context and given the chance, what improvements would you have made?'

'Yes, you've obviously given a deal of thought to this aspect

Short-listing and interview techniques 83

– so, just to put me in the picture, why didn't you proceed along these lines?'

'I see. Tell me, if asked, how would you describe your style of management?'

'Well, if I may say, that's a pretty frank self-appraisal. . . . Now, with the benefit of hindsight, how do you think this went down with the people at Fisher's – firstly, where your subordinates were concerned?'

'And what about your boss – how did he view your management style?'

'It was ever thus! Now, changing the subject, what do you regard as your most significant achievement at Fisher's?'

'Please tell me more – why was that, do you think?'

'And, again, with the benefit of hindsight, what would you say was the *least* successful aspect of your performance?'

'Well, there's one thing for sure – we can't win them all! Finally, in round terms, how would you say that your time at Fisher's has served your overall career objectives?'

Probing a candidate's leisure activities

'Let's turn to the question of what you do with yourself in your spare time. . . . I see that hang-gliding's at the head of your list – now, that really interests me. Tell me, in a few words, if you had to take a group of learners in this activity, how would you organize their initial training?'

'Hum, I somehow think I'd never make the grade! What's your depth of involvement in the sport – for instance, how often do you manage to get airborne?'

'And what about this yen for DIY – which, incidentally, I envy – tell me more about this activity.'

'What do you reckon has been your most significant DIY achievement to date?'

'Hey, that's splendid. . . . I see you've also mentioned

84 *The Secrets of Successful Hiring and Firing*

reading as a leisure pursuit – what are your particular tastes?'

'I see. . . . Who would you recommend as a first-rate author in this field?'

'Really, that's interesting – why, exactly?'

'Fine, you obviously enjoy your reading! Given the opportunity, what other spare time activity would you like to take up?'

'Why that choice?'

'So, if you'll forgive me, why haven't you taken it up?'

Probing important requirements

(*Preamble*) 'Now, while I appreciate that you've completed all the relevant sections in the application form, there are certain important questions which I must again put to you – this time, face-to-face. . . . All right?'

'Good. . . . First, and discounting any offences which are "spent" under the provisions of the Rehabilitation of Offenders Act 1974, you've certified that you have had no criminal convictions. . . . My question is, what do you now wish to tell me that may prevent you suffering embarrassment in the event that we take any clearance action deemed necessary?' (Note: *Most business organizations have no official right, or means, to undertake this form of 'clearance' – but, phrased as suggested, the question constitutes a useful, investigative ploy.*)

'Fine – thank you for being so forthright. Second, I note from the medical questionnaire that you've certified to the effect that you've never been seriously ill, or undergone any surgical treatment. . . . So, what I must ask you is, what d'you now wish to tell me that may prevent any embarrassment to you in the event that we require you to undergo a full medical examination?' (Note: *The question may, of*

Short-listing and interview techniques 85

course, be a prelude to an actual examination – but, even when this is not the case, it is, once again, a useful, investigative ploy.)

'In your own interest, it's necessary for me to remind you that you've certified to the effect that all the facts given in support of your application are true. This being so, what d'you now wish to tell me that may prevent any embarrassment to you as a result of our routine enquiries?'

In looking over this 'interview sampler', remember that its prime purpose is to set you thinking about the overall effectiveness of the questions *you* habitually pose at interview. If there are such things as endemic interviewing weaknesses (and, by now, you should have got the message that there's a positive army of them), one such beast is certainly the innate reluctance of interviewers to study and improve their questioning technique – so, once more unto the breach, my friend, once more!

THE ALL-ESSENTIAL ASSESSMENT BIT

It's no earthly use being a bright-eyed, bushy-tailed, proficient interviewer if, at the same time, you're prone to tumbling at the very next fence in the selection handicap – the assessment stage. In addition to the vital need to set aside time for candidate assessment immediately after each and every interview, there is the equally vital requirement to employ a *standard set of yardsticks against which all interviewees will be measured*. I offer one such approach for your consideration.

A POST-INTERVIEW ASSESSMENT PROCEDURE

Rate each candidate in respect of the following criteria:

1 Why is the applicant interested in the vacancy?

86 *The Secrets of Successful Hiring and Firing*

2 Why is he seeking another post?
3 What has he discovered about your organization?
4 Could he have easily discovered more than this if he had shown more interest?
5 Why has he left previous jobs? Is there likely to be an undesirable repetition in the future?
6 Will his short-term career aims be satisfied by your job?
7 Will the job fit in with his long-term career objectives?
8 Has the applicant followed a definite career pattern to date – and realized his earlier aims?
9 Does your job constitute a *logical* progression of his career?
10 Are you confident that his personal strengths are consistent with the major demands of your job?
11 How do you view his apparent limitations and weaknesses in relation to your job?
12 Has he asked intelligent and searching questions about the company, the job and the associated conditions of employment?
13 Are you confident that the applicant's qualifications and experience are adequate for the job?
14 Are his manner, speech and attitudes suited to the job?
15 Or were they deliberately assumed for the selection process – i.e., is he a sham?
16 Will he be able to work in sufficient harmony with prospective colleagues?

AND, FINALLY, HOW TO REJECT THE UNWANTED

If you are to foster and maintain your company's reputation as a decent employer, it behoves you to give a deal of serious thought to the manner in which you *reject* unwanted candidates – for, rest assured, these sundry unfortunates will certainly spread the word about the treatment they receive at your hands. So, be brief, but be kind:

Example of a rejection letter

Dear Mr Horrocks

We have now completed our selection for the post of Credit Control Clerk and, sadly, I have to inform you that your application has not been successful on this occasion.

In expressing the hope that this will not be too much of a disappointment, I would like to thank you for your very considerable interest – and, of course, add my very best wishes for your eventual success.

Yours sincerely

And that's that – happy interviewing!

5   Processing the lucky ones
How to rope them in – and make them stay

We can now sigh with relief. . . . Having selected our bright-eyed, bushy-tailed candidate for this or that job, it only remains to bring the lucky so-and-so into the fold. So, without further ado, let's think in terms of that glorious communication, the written offer of employment.

IRONCLAD CORSETS LTD

Whalebone House, Croup Lane, Whittlesey, Cambs PE27 1NN

Our ref: 352/12 Pers
Your ref:

15 January 1988

Miss B T Carruthers
13 Twitchett Way
Bury
Huntingdon PE17 9GD

Dear Miss Carruthers

Following your interview of last Monday, I am pleased to offer you the post of Finishing Room Supervisor within this company, commencing 2 February 1988.

I enclose two copies of the statement of the particulars of employment for the post, and should be much obliged if you would confirm your acceptance of this offer by signing and returning one copy to me as soon as possible.

90 The Secrets of Successful Hiring and Firing

I look forward to welcoming you to the company at 9.00 a.m. on 2 February, and to the start of what I am confident will be a long and mutually beneficial association.

Yours sincerely

Harold B Thrups
General Manager

Plainly, the meat in that letter-sandwich is, as always, the bit in the middle – for it smacks of the law. Now, while it would be an insult to offer that managers are an irresponsible lot, there is little doubt that many of us tend to shy away and hide under the bedclothes when faced with any process which, horror of horrors, carries legal overtones. And, yes, our endemic attitude to the formalities of employment documentation is a case in point; as witness:

‘What was that – a written statement of, er, particulars of employment? Never heard of it. . . .’

‘Contract of employment, d’you say? Ah, yes, you mean the letter offering the job – of course, we use ’em. . . .’

‘Look, we just don’t have the time for all that nonsense – and, anyway, we’ve never had any trouble with our lot. . . .

Let’s face it, these days, people are only too pleased to land a job – they’re not the slightest bit interested in a bloody great load of red tape. . . .’

These are just some of the acerbic comments made by manager-students during an in-company training session.

Be all that as it may. . . . So far as you are concerned, reader, I shall assume that, since you are reading this book, I’m preaching to the good old converted! So, with no further ado, let’s remind ourselves of the legal significance of that middle paragraph in our sample offer of employment:

'I enclose two copies of the *statement of the particulars of employment for the post,* and should be obliged if you would *confirm your acceptance of this offer by signing and returning one copy to me* as soon as possible.'

WRITTEN STATEMENTS OF PARTICULARS OF EMPLOYMENT

Under British law (currently the Employment Protection [Consolidation] Act 1978), all employees who work for sixteen or more hours per week are entitled to receive written particulars of the main terms of their employment *within thirteen weeks of being engaged.* The minimum details specified by the legal-beagles for inclusion in a written statement are:

(a) The names of the employer and the employee.
(b) The date of commencement of the employment.
(c) The date on which the employee's period of continuous service began.
(d) The employee's job title.
(e) The rate or method of calculating pay (which must include details of overtime pay, commission, bonus, etc.).
(f) The intervals at which remuneration is paid.
(g) The hours of work.
(h) Details of annual/public holiday entitlements, holiday pay (including any entitlement to accrued holiday pay on leaving the employment).
(i) Details of any conditions relating to sick leave and sick pay.
(j) Details of any entitlement to membership of a pension scheme.
(k) The periods of notice to be given by either side.
(l) The job title of the person to whom the employee can apply if he or she wishes to appeal against any

92 *The Secrets of Successful Hiring and Firing*

       disciplinary decision, and how such application should be made.

(m) The job title of the person to whom the employee can apply if he or she wishes to seek redress of any grievance relating to the employment, and how such application should be made.

(n) Whether or not a contracting-out certificate issued under the Social Security Pensions Act 1975 is in force for the employment concerned.

In an effort to ease your way, I have included a sample statement of particulars of employment in Appendix 2.

SO WHY OBTAIN THE POTENTIAL EMPLOYEE'S SIGNATURE ON THE STATEMENT?

The reasons for adding an employee's signature block to the statement of particulars of employment are two-fold – it all depends on the wording of the certificate. On the one hand, the dyed-in-the-wool administrator may merely wish to arm himself with evidence that the statement has been received, in which case a simple sentence, 'I acknowledge receipt of a copy of the above statement', would suffice. On the other hand, it may well be that the employer wishes the statement to double as a written contract of employment, in which case such words as, 'I agree to the above terms and conditions of my employment', would fill the bill. If, however, you are considering the latter alternative (or, for that matter, if you are thinking of issuing contracts of employment in addition to written statements), then the next section is for you.

CONTRACTS OF EMPLOYMENT

There is no requirement in British law for a contract of

employment to be in writing, but despite this oft-convenient let-out and as I've already mentioned, some employers seem to favour issuing written statements in the form of contracts. This is all hunky-dory, *provided* that the 'combined document' is far more extensive in its detail than a written statement – for the important reason that a contract of employment must include *all* the terms and conditions to which the parties have agreed, not merely the minimum information prescribed by law for statements. So, my advice is, if you're thinking in any context about the issue of written contracts, bring the company solicitor into the act.

PROBATION IS ALL ABOUT BEING FAIR . . .

Mention the word 'probation' and a whole army of Blighty-based, rapscallion employers (present company excepted, I hope) will well-nigh cackle with glee:

> *'Ho, ho, probation, you say? Why, me dear chap, these days, we don't have to worry about taking 'em on probation – the law's done it all for us! Just think about it. . . . One can't be done for unfair dismissal if a character's had less than two years' service – right? Well, then, that means that anyone we take on is automatically on two years' probation, doesn't it? Don't bother with all this nonsense about TELLING 'em they're on probation – just give 'm the bloody kick before the two years are up, and Bob's your uncle!'*

With that all said and done, let's take a glance at the manner in which a caring and responsible employer will treat probation. First, *at the time of his engagement*, a probationary employee will be made well aware that he is on trial for a stated period – and that, during this period, it is largely up to him to establish his suitability for continued employment. At the same time, the boss will recognize his inescapable responsibility to provide adequate training, to

94 The Secrets of Successful Hiring and Firing

nurture the probationer throughout – and, of course, to draw any shortcomings to the guy or gal's attention.

Since none of us are perfect selectors, there's bound to be the odd, unfortunate occasion when a probationer falls down on the job – to the extent that, despite having been given every opportunity to improve, a scrupulous investigation confirms that dismissal is the only alternative. When this proves to be the case, our caring employer will ensure that the person concerned is provided with the minimum period of statutory notice (of which more anon in Part Two), or pay in lieu of notice, and sent on his way.

Yes, probation *is* all about being fair, isn't it?

THEY CALL IT INDUCTION TRAINING

Situated not too far from where I sit writing these words, there's an otherwise kindly employer of some 250 people who has plainly never even heard of induction training. Displaying the unmistakable signs of ad hoc expansion, his factory sprawls untidily across an extensive, confusing site and – well, you can guess what's coming. That's right, whenever a new employee (often a school-leaver) turns up for that stressful first day, the poor character is literally pitchforked into the deep end – left to his or her own devices to navigate the place; find out where the canteen, the loo and goodness knows what-all are situated; learn by inquiry how pay is issued, who looks after first aid; and, in pretty big sum, what's what and who's who. Unintentional or not, this is no way to treat any new employee, particularly a youngster – and, whatever the the size of the outfit concerned, there is simply no excuse for failing to implement adequate induction training; for example, embracing:

(a) A brief account of the firm's function, history and aims for the future, preferably delivered by a senior manager (why not prise Big Daddy from that lofty perch – the descent to reality should do him good).

Processing the lucky ones 95

(b) A conducted tour of the premises – and, if it's a complex site, provision of a map with all the essentials clearly marked.

(c) A talk by someone from personnel; outlining arrangements for pay, clocking on and off, arrangements for refreshment, disciplinary and grievance procedures, welfare, etc. – together with the provision of an employees' handbook containing all such information, presented in an easily digestible and attractive form.

(d) A talk by a suitably qualified person on matters of health and safety.

(e) An introduction to the new employee's direct boss, if still required, and work colleagues.

(f) And, after all the above, any job training that is deemed necessary.

I make no apology for adding that, in addition to ensuring the all-round proficiency of a new employee, properly conducted induction training makes them not only feel at home, but *wanted*, to boot. And that, if you like, is the last big secret of successful hiring. . . .

Part Two   Firing

6 Dismissal – another essential preamble
This, you wretch, is the quick bullet

Once upon a time, as they say – in the days of old, when bosses were bold, and governments weren't invented, tra la – every employer had the divine right to fire anyone he liked, whenever he liked, for whatever reason he liked. And, lest you feel like weeping for the glorious past, let me remind you that today's Big Daddy still enjoys this handy prerogative. However, in this sceptred isle, there's a twentieth-century complication – he may have to pay for the privilege. And how. . . . To put it in Lewis Carroll's inimitable way, it's not the Jabberwock with jaws to bite and claws to catch, or the frumious Bandersnatch, that British bosses have to fear – oh, no, dismissal-wise, the thing that goes bump in the night is that government-created scourge of mismanagement, the industrial tribunal.

While, for certain, the burgeoning advent of law on employment protection has not been confined to the UK, it could be that you, reader, earn your daily bread in some far-flung spot where the legal reins have yet to be applied. If this is the case, you may feel inclined to thank your lucky stars, but do read on – for, law or no law, what follows is all about wielding the dismissal axe efficiently and *fairly*. And that, me overseas bucko, concerns you just as much as your striving counterparts back here in Blighty.

100   *The Secrets of Successful Hiring and Firing*

So, casting geography aside, let's get on with it.

THE CRUX OF THE MATTER

When a boss is faced with a situation so serious that firing this or that employee appears to be the only possible alternative, it behoves him to remember that this is an utterly drastic course of action. I use the term 'drastic' simply because any action that can possibly result in the ruination of someone's life just has to bear such a tag. Sadly, and as many of us know to our cost, there are those bosses who, in their arrogance, fail to consider dismissal in this light:

> *'Yes, that's right – I sacked him. . . . What did you expect me to say – that I gave the so-and-so a pat on the back and told him to be a good boy in future? Look, I'm a businessman, not a bloody philanthropist. . . . My people know the score, well enough – one step out of line, and that's it. . . .'*

A conversation-stopper comment made by a small-time employer during, of all things, a seminar on unfair dismissal.

> *'That's all very well – but if you had to put up with some of the good-for-nothings that I'm saddled with, you'd soon change your tune. . . . They're just out for all they can get – and couldn't care less about putting in a fair day's work. There's only one answer to that kind of attitude – hit 'em, and hit 'em hard. . . . After all, it's my business and I'm the one who carries the can. . . .'*

An extract from a taped discussion with an 'I-came-up-the-hard-way' restaurant proprietor.

> *'To hell with what the law says – I made my business what it is today, and, with all due respect, no damned do-gooder's going to tell me how to run it. . . . What's more, I haven't*

Dismissal – another essential preamble 101

got the time or the inclination to put up with any nonsense from my lot – if they put a foot wrong, that's their misfortune, not mine.'

A fiery observation made by the owner of a very successful road haulage firm.

Now, before you start breathing fire, I haven't got an outsize chip on my shoulder and I do believe that the sanction of dismissal, albeit a drastic measure, is a necessary weapon in any employer's armoury. Having stated thus, I make no apology whatsoever for proceeding to put the boot in. . . . When confronted with a potential dismissal situation, far too many managers fail to ask themselves the one, all-important question:

IN THE LIGHT OF *ALL* THE CIRCUMSTANCES AND CASTING ASIDE ALL EMOTIVE THOUGHT, WOULD A DECISION TO DISMISS BE THE ACTION OF A *REASONABLE* EMPLOYER?

In its wisdom, the Court of Appeal has expanded on this vital theme:

'A very important factor of which he (the employer) *has to take account, on the facts known to him at that time, is whether there will or will not be injustice to the employee and the extent of that injustice. For example, he will clearly have to take account of the length of time during which the employee has been employed by him, the satisfactoriness or otherwise of the employee's service, the difficulties which may face the employee in obtaining other employment, and matters of that sort. None of these is decisive, but they are all matters which affect the justice or injustice to the employee of being dismissed.'*

Dobie v Burns International Security Services (UK) Ltd (1984) IRLR 329.

Note, especially, the court's words, *'the difficulties which*

102 *The Secrets of Successful Hiring and Firing*

may face the employee in obtaining other employment. . . .' – and ask yourself, how many employers seriously consider this aspect before firing the quick bullet? And, of all the bosses who do think of it, how many of them speedily squash such thoughts with an emotive, 'Ah, but, then – he had it coming to him,' or similar sentiment?

Dismissal is, or should be, one of the several culminations of a thoroughly fair, investigative system. Now, I'll take it for granted that your organization has a well-established and published disciplinary procedure★, but have you ever thought of giving it the once-over for woodworm, and the like?

TIPS FOR CHECKING A DISCIPLINARY PROCEDURE

1 The procedure will almost certainly refer (well, doesn't it?) to the need for an investigation into any alleged offence or shortcoming. Okay, go to the appropriate filing cabinet and drag out the record of a past dismissal. Examine the paperwork. Does it reflect the labours of a thorough investigation – or, just perchance, is there little or *no* flaming paperwork? If the latter is the case, don't despair – we'll be dealing with this crucial aspect a bit later on. For the present, suffice it to say that there's something mightily amiss with your much-vaunted procedure. And, by the way, are you happy that there *was* a full investigation in the case concerned?

2 The prescribed disciplinary hearing. . . . I've no doubt (that's a lie) that your procedure lays down the law on who should attend the hearing; witnesses, the em-

---

★ *On second thoughts, I jolly well won't take it for granted. . . . The UK Advisory, Conciliation and Arbitration Service (ACAS) has produced an excellent Code of Practice which I recommend to any miscreant employer who has yet to set up a disciplinary procedure. Entitled 'Disciplinary Practice and Procedures in Employment', it can be obtained from ACAS at 11–12 St James's Square, London SW1Y 4LA. If the cap happens to fit, reader, get thee to a nunnery – and start swotting-up the Code.*

Dismissal – another essential preamble 103

ployee's representative, and so on – but does it go into detail, say, on the following requirements?

Provision of a written notice to the employee:

- Informing him that a formal hearing will be held, and when.
- Reminding him of his rights at the hearing regarding witnesses, employee's representative, presentation of his case, etc.
- Ensuring that he will be in no doubt about the possible consequences of the hearing (acceptance of his side of the story, the range of penalties, etc.).

3 Your procedure should refer to the fact that any formal reprimand will be expunged from an employee's personnel record after a defined period of satisfactory service. Check around – are they actually being erased and forgotten, as promised? The proof of this particular pudding is that you should find no trace at all of them. . . .

Enough of disciplinary procedures for now – remembering that this is a scene-setting chapter, let's get back to the square-one basics of dismissal.

A NOTE ON SUMMARY DISMISSAL

Summary or instant dismissal is the employer's ultimate sanction and is rightly confined to cases of gross misconduct, of which more anon. Oddly enough, I've come across quite a number of bosses who, having told me about this or that 'summary dismissal', then fell over backwards to inform me that they gave pay in lieu of notice to the employees concerned! I'm not sure whether they were trying to temper justice with mercy, or were merely suffering from a stiff dose of cowardice – but, whatever their motives, they would do well to note that the very essence of summary dismissal is that no notice pay *is* payable.

104   *The Secrets of Successful Hiring and Firing*

Apropos of tribunal complaints, it's also wise to remember that the longer a boss takes to make up his mind over a case, the weaker his position may become if, indeed, he does decide to summarily dismiss the wrongdoer.

SO WHAT ABOUT THOSE PERIODS OF NOTICE?

In this country, the statutory minimum periods of notice★ to be given by employers are as follows:

Period of continuous service	*Requisite minimum notice*
One month or more, but under two years	One week
Two years or more, but under twelve years	One week for each year of continuous service
Twelve years or more	Twelve weeks

If an employee's contract of employment specifies a longer period of notice, then the employer is contractually bound to give that longer period. In the event that a hard-nut boss refuses to honour such a contractual obligation, it's open to conjecture whether or not the aggrieved person would go to the trouble and expense of seeking a remedy – by way of a civil court action for damages.

SOMETHING ON THAT NEBULOUS THING, CONSTRUCTIVE DISMISSAL

Again, in Blighty, if an employee considers that his boss has made his working conditions so intolerable that he has no alternative but to resign, and if he does resign, he may complain to an industrial tribunal that he's been *constructively dismissed*. In other words, it is alleged that, by thus forcing his victim's hand, the scallywag employer has taken

★ *Vide s.49 of the Employment Protection (Consolidation) Act 1978. The Act also lists the odd-ball employees who are excluded from entitlement to minimum periods of notice.*

Dismissal – another essential preamble 105

action which is tantamount to dismissal – without actually going through the motions.

However, the employee who decides to tread this rocky path to justice will have no hope of success unless he can show that:

- His employer's conduct was so bad that he was not only forced, but *entitled* to leave – and, also, entitled to terminate his employment without notice.
- Inter alia, his employer is guilty of conduct which (*according to a Court of Appeal dictum**) 'is a significant breach going to the root of the contract of employment', and 'shows that the employer no longer intends to be bound by one or more of the essential terms of the contract'.

So, in the light of these requirements, it's likely that the traditional opener, 'He wanted me out because my face didn't fit,' will need a whole heap of cogent supporting evidence to make an allegation of constructive dismissal stand any chance of success.

And, anyway, boss-reader, you wouldn't get up to such knavish tricks – would you?

SUSPENSION CAN BE A GOOD IDEA, BUT . . .

When things do go wrong and it is necessary for a manager to investigate a serious disciplinary case, it's often a good idea to suspend the alleged offender from work pending the outcome of the investigation. But, be warned, there is a pitfall to be avoided – never suspend an employee on less than full pay unless such action is clearly provided for in the man or woman's contract of employment. The guideline is

* *The keen reader may wish to study the pearly words of Lord Denning, when Master of the Rolls, in Western Excavating (ECC) Ltd v Sharp (1978) IRLR 27. He may also wish to peruse a further explanation of this bit of law in the case of Sparfax Ltd v Harrison (1980) IRLR 442. Incidentally, any public library will obtain copies of the Industrial Relations Law Reports for reference use.*

quite simple: an employer's contractual obligation to pay an employee does not extend to an obligation to provide work.★ So, if the contract of employment says nothing about suspension on less than full pay, send the accused home without financial penalty – and don't try to dock the money from his or her accrued holiday pay. . . .

I suggest you take a wee break before plunging into the next chapter – go on, you've earned it.

★ *Just in case you are overflowing with zeal and energy, the case precedent for this right little gem is Turner v Sawdon and Co. (1901) 2 KB 653.*

7 Dismissing the baddies and the failures

Let the punishment fit the crime

If you'll forgive an old ex-Serviceman his reminiscence, one of the handiest aids to wielding discipline within the RAF was – and probably still is – that second-only-to-the-Bible tome, the *Manual of Air Force Law*. While it's a very long time since I last had occasion to thumb through its pages, I distinctly recall that the good old MAFL not only provided a comprehensive list of offences and associated maximum punishments, but also nursed its reader through super-detailed instructions on how to crack the disciplinary whip in each and every case. The point I'm making is that, more often than not, the executive knapsacks of those in business and industry contain no such idiot's guide – with the almost inevitable result that far too many of us drop whip-wielding clangers right, left and centre.

So, let's set about replacing at least part of the vacuum with some hints and tips for survival in this discipline-jungle.

DISMISSAL FOR MISCONDUCT

While most employees' manuals make lip-smacking reference to fighting, drinking, stealing and so on as examples of gross misconduct punishable by dismissal, the really basic

110 *The Secrets of Successful Hiring and Firing*

questions are usually left unanswered – and, since we've got to start somewhere, it mightn't be a bad idea to take a look at some of them.

Q *First, let's get one thing straight – in the eyes of the law, what constitutes common or garden misconduct?*

A Any act or behaviour which, although punishable, would not normally result in the dismissal of the employee concerned.

Q *And what about instances of misconduct committed outside work – how does the law view these?*

A The Employment Appeals Tribunal has really come up to scratch on this one:

> *Conduct does not have to be something which occurs in the course of the actual work, or at the actual place of work, or even to be connected with the work, so long as in some respect or other it affects the employee, or could be thought to be likely to affect the employee, when he is doing his work.*
>
> *Singh v London Country Bus Service Ltd (1976) ITR 131*

Q *What constitutes gross misconduct?*

A Any act or behaviour by an employee which *fundamentally breaches his or her contract of employment*, thereby justifying summary dismissal.

Q *How do I decide whether a particular offence does, in fact, constitute gross misconduct?*

A Often, with some difficulty. . . . A safety-first test is to ask yourself the $64,000 question, 'Striving to ignore my gut-reaction to the offence *and* any emotive feelings I may have about the employee concerned, is it even slightly on the cards that someone else dealing impartially with the case would deem a formal warning to be sufficient?' If your response is in the affirmative or you feel the slightest uncertainty, then you're probably batting on a very sticky wicket – and it would be wise to treat the offence as straightforward misconduct.

Dismissing the baddies and the failures 111

A further, somewhat belt-and-braces test is to consider in all honesty whether, having been adjudged guilty of the offence, the continued presence of the employee at work would be *wholly intolerable*. Needless to add, such consideration presupposes that a full and fair hearing has taken place. . . . Plainly, if there is any uncertainty in the matter, it follows that the employee must be given the benefit of the doubt.

Q *In cases of gross misconduct, can I take my time in arriving at what, by any standards, is a very serious decision?*

A While precipitate, ill-considered action is obviously to be avoided like the plague, there must be no undue delay in investigating and adjudging any offence – *particularly* when it constitutes gross misconduct. Moreover, the employee concerned should always be suspended from work pending the all-important decision – for, if he is permitted to remain at his post and is *then* subsequently dismissed, the employer's case that gross misconduct has occurred may be deemed by a tribunal to have been substantially weakened. . . . Similarly, any undue delay in resolving such serious disciplinary matters will almost certainly incur a tribunal's displeasure – so speedy but meticulous action is of the essence.

Q *Okay, now say I do dismiss an employee for gross misconduct. Are there any guidelines on how a tribunal may subsequently examine my action?*

A Well, yes, some. . . . In essence, the Court of Appeal has recommended that:

- The employer must demonstrate that he had reasonable grounds for dismissing the employee.
- The employer must also demonstrate that he acted reasonably in the circumstances, having regard to equity and the substantial merits of the case.
- Equity will not be served if the employee is denied a fair opportunity of explaining why he committed the offence before he is dismissed, or if the

employer forms hasty, ill-founded conclusions about the employee's misconduct.

The above is merely a summary of the Court of Appeal recommendations – for chapter and verse, the wise manager will fly to *W. Weddel and Co. Ltd v Tepper (1980) IRLR 96.*

The Employment Appeals Tribunal has also made some recommendations which are highly relevant to this thorny topic:

What the tribunal have to decide every time is, broadly expressed, whether the employer who discharged the employee on the ground of the misconduct in question (usually, though not necessarily, dishonest conduct) entertained a reasonable suspicion amounting to a belief in the guilt of the employee of that misconduct at that time. That is really stating shortly and compendiously what is in fact more than one element. First of all, there must be established by the employer the fact of that belief; that the employer did believe it. Second, that the employer had in his mind reasonable grounds upon which to sustain that belief. And third, we think, that the employer, at the stage at which he formed that belief on those grounds, at any rate at the final stage at which he formed that belief on those grounds, had carried out as much investigation into the matter as was reasonable in all the circumstances of the case. It is the employer who manages to discharge the onus of demonstrating these three matters, we think, who must not be examined further. It is not relevant, as we think, that the tribunal would itself have shared that view in those circumstances. It is not relevant, as we think, for the tribunal to examine the quality of the material which the employer had before him, for instance to see whether it was the sort of material, objectively considered, which would lead to a certain conclusion on the balance of probabilities, or whether it was the sort of material which would lead to the same conclusion only upon the basis of being 'sure' as it is now said more normally in a criminal context, or, to use the more old-fashioned term, such as to put the matter 'beyond reasonable doubt'. The test, and the test all the way through, is reasonableness; and certainly, as it seems to us, a conclusion on the balance of probabilities will in any surmisable circumstance be a reasonable conclusion.

British Home Stores Ltd v Burchell (1978) IRLR 379

While the EAT has indicated that tribunals should regard all the above points as recommendations, so far as you and I at the exposed, sharp end are concerned – well, maybe, a nod's as good as a wink.

FOR GOODNESS SAKE, WHAT ABOUT SOME DOWN-TO-EARTH, *PRACTICAL* HELP?

All right, I hear you call – and here, in note form, are some hints concerning the more common instances of gross misconduct.

Offence	*Notes*
Fighting	1 For the record, we're thinking in terms of fighting and any other form of violence or threats of violence.
	2 Never make the error of regarding fighting (etc.) as an offence warranting *automatic* dismissal – it *must* be fully investigated (remember that vital bit, 'having regard to equity and the substantial merits of the case'?).
	3 Among other things, the investigation should seek to establish the

extent, if any, of provocation or reasonable action taken by the employee to defend himself against unprovoked attack, etc.

Drinking/ drunkenness

1 Remember, again, that the existence of a company rule prohibiting drinking or drunkenness on pain of instant dismissal does *not* mean that automatic dismissal is warranted.

2 Notwithstanding the reminder at 1, above, it is advisable for the employer to strengthen his position by having such a rule.

3 The employee should always be suspended until such time as he is fully sober and fit to attend the disciplinary hearing.

4 The investigation should include consideration of:

(a) Specific evidence that the employee concerned was, indeed, under the influence of alcohol.

(b) The position and status of the employee, with particular reference to his authority and responsibilities.

(c) The nature of the employee's job and the overall risks occasioned by any incapability due to drinking/ drunkenness.

(d) The employee's explanation of his conduct.

Dismissing the baddies and the failures 115

Stealing and other criminal offences	1	It is *not* correct that an employer is obliged (or even advised) to suspend his disciplinary proceedings pending the outcome of any criminal court action. In all such cases, the *Burchell* test (see earlier in this chapter) should be applied and action taken, accordingly. Plainly, if, as a result of applying the *Burchell* test, it is clear that insufficient grounds exist on which to form a reasonable belief in the employee's guilt, then suspension pending the outcome of any court case *is* advisable.
	2	In cases where the police are investigating an alleged offence, it sometimes happens that the employer is asked to 'hold off' taking any action; i.e., refrain from interviewing the employee concerned or holding any inquiry. Since, in the vast majority of such cases (always remembering the vitality of the *Burchell* test), there is no real risk that an investigation by the employer will prejudice the matter, it might be wise to consult a senior police officer – reminding that worthy of the consequences (in terms of the business, in general, and employee morale, in particular) of delaying any internal disciplinary action. If the police remain adamant in their view, it might then be a good idea for the

employer to enlist the aid of the company solicitor – who should not need reminding that the judgement *R v BBC ex parte Lavelle (1982) IRLR 404* is relevant. . . .

NOW, WHAT ABOUT DISMISSAL ON THE GROUNDS OF 'TOTTED-UP' OFFENCES?

Sadly, it often transpires that an employee who has committed one or more acts of 'simple' misconduct chooses to ignore any previous warnings – and, bingo, perpetrates a further sin. On this occasion, however, the boss has had enough and, mindful of the beggar's culminative misbehaviour, dismisses him (or her – mustn't forget the ladies) on the spot. Even more sadly, it often transpires that the sacked employee proceeds at a gallop to the ever-handy tribunal – and yet another dollop of you-know-what hits the fan. Sadder still to relate, the immutable provisions of Sod's Law dictate that, just sometimes, such complaints of unfair dismissal are crowned with success – and, who knows, there but for the grace of the Great Chairman in the Sky. . . . So, it now behoves us to examine the various pitfalls that await the manager who treads this particularly stony path.

Whenever an employee's conduct warrants a formal warning, this should be issued in writing – see Figure 10 for a typical example.

You will note that Figure 10 typifies a 'first' formal warning. Given the necessary amendment, it will suffice for any ensuing warnings – with, of course, the important exception of the final ultimatum, which is exemplified at Figure 11.

Now, reader, if you're the caring manager I think you are, you can skip the next few lines – because they're directed at the scallywag who believes there's little harm in

Dismissing the baddies and the failures 117

NOTICE OF FORMAL WARNING

To **Mr D. Incarnate** *Job Title* **Operative (Gd II)**

Dept **Production**   *Date* **17 February 1988**

The purpose of this notice is to confirm that at a disciplinary hearing held earlier today you were adjudged guilty of misconduct; in that:

at approximately 10.15 a.m. on 17 February 1988, you were observed by Mr B. A. Eyesight, the Production Supervisor, to be drinking from a can of beer while carrying out your assigned work — an act which was in flagrant breach of company regulations.

After full consideration of this matter, you are now warned that any repetition of misconduct on your part will place your continued employment with this company at risk. This warning constitutes the first formal stage of the company's disciplinary procedure. It will be recorded in your personnel record and will remain there for three months, after which it will be expunged provided that your conduct has been satisfactory during this time. You have a right of appeal against this warning. If you wish to exercise this right, you should address your appeal, within seven days of the date of this notice, to the Production Director.

B. R. Hughes
Production Manager

Figure 10 *A typical formal warning in respect of misconduct*

118   *The Secrets of Successful Hiring and Firing*

NOTICE OF FINAL WARNING

To
Mr D. Incarnate   *Job Title*   **Operative (Gd II)**

Dept **Production**   *Date* **14 April 1988**

The purpose of this notice is to confirm that at a disciplinary hearing held earlier today you were adjudged guilty of misconduct; in that:

> **at approximately 12.15 p.m. on 13 April 1988, you were observed by Mr B. A. Eyesight, the Production Supervisor, to be smoking a cigarette while working in the Cellulose Paint Store, a clearly-marked 'No Smoking' area — an act which was in flagrant breach of company regulations.**

After full consideration of this matter, you are now warned that any repetition of misconduct on your part will render you liable to dismissal without further warning. This warning constitutes the second formal stage of the company's disciplinary procedure. It will be recorded in your personnel record and will remain there for three months, after which it will be expunged provided that your conduct has been satisfactory during this time. You have a right of appeal against this warning. If you wish to exercise this right, you should address your appeal, within seven days of the date of this notice, to the Production Director.

B. R. Hughes
Production Manager

Figure 11   *A typical final warning in respect of misconduct*

driving a horse and cart through the principles of fair play. So, stand by for blasting. . . . When a formal warning states that after a given period it will be expunged, *then that is exactly what it means*. There's a name for the act of erasing an offence from the record and simultaneously engraving it on one's heart – yes, that's right, we call it bearing a grudge. And, by the way, the idiot disciplinarian who attempts to resurrect a 'spent offence' as part and parcel of a dismissal package is really bucking for trouble. . . .

Which brings us to the crunch. Unfortunately, there will always be the odd employee who, despite previous warnings, is determined to bring about his or her own downfall – and thus it is that, one day, you'll certainly be faced with the unpleasantly thorny business of firing a quick bullet. But do remember that the dismissal blunderbuss has a nasty habit of back-firing in one's face, so prime your weapon with care. Always ensure that:

- Previous warnings are firmly on the record and that, in each and every instance, the employee concerned was given an opportunity to mend his ways.
- The employee fully understands the facts of the case against him.
- Immediately prior to the pronouncement of dismissal, the employee is given a final chance to explain his conduct.
- The pronouncement of dismissal is accompanied by a full verbal explanation of the procedure for appeal.
- The employee is requested to acknowledge receipt of the formal notice of dismissal by signing a copy thereof (see the example in Figure 12).

DISMISSAL RELATED TO CAPABILITY AND/ OR QUALIFICATIONS

I think you may agree that when an industrial tribunal is faced with a case involving dismissal for lack of capability

120 *The Secrets of Successful Hiring and Firing*

NOTIFICATION OF SUMMARY DISMISSAL

To   Mr D. Incarnate   *Job Title*   Operative (Gd II)

***Dept* Production**   ***Date* 2 June 1988**

Brief details and date of offence

At approximately 4.45 p.m. on 2 June 1988, you were informed by Mr B. A. Eyesight, the Production Supervisor, that the work you had carried out on Job No. 3521 was sub-standard. Your reply to this legitimate criticism was couched in highly offensive terms, and you were accordingly informed by Mr Eyesight that you would be reported for misconduct.

After full consideration of this matter at a disciplinary hearing held today, you were adjudged guilty of misconduct and, taking into account the formal warning issued to you on 14 April 1987, you are therefore dismissed from the company's employment with immediate effect. If you consider that you have been wrongly dismissed you have the right to appeal. If you wish to exercise this right, you should address your appeal in writing, within three working days of your dismissal, to the Production Director.

You are requested to acknowledge receipt of this notification of summary dismissal by signing the duplicate copy.

B. R. Hughes
Production Manager

I acknowledge receipt of a copy of this notification.

Signed .... **Date** .

Figure 12   *A typical notification of summary dismissal for misconduct*

Dismissing the baddies and the failures 121

and/or qualifications, they'll pose the employer a right blockbuster of a metaphorical question; namely:

'If, as you would have us believe, you are a responsible organization, we must assume that you exercised great care when initially selecting the applicant for this employment. . . . *Pray tell us, if he was suitable at the start, how did it subsequently come about that you deemed him so incapable as to warrant his dismissal?*'

All right, tongue-in-cheek approach that may be, but the fact remains that many employers utilize peanut-type selection methods – and then wield the dismissal axe like fury when they find themselves saddled with monkeys. Still, it's beyond my terms of reference to dwell on such matters as stinking selection at the recruitment stage (or, for that matter, boringly repetitive confirmation of the Peter Principle by persisting to promote employees to the levels of their incompetence), so I'd better get back on track. Er, sorry about that.

It's the duty of every manager to monitor the perform-ance of each of his subordinates and, when deficiencies are revealed, to make every possible effort to correct these by dint of effective training, helpful discussion and, would you believe, sympathetic counselling. Or, to put it another way, it's *not* a manager's duty to detect shortcomings in performance and, assuming the role of Machiavelli, wade in with accusations and warnings of incapability without, first, having a damned good crack at what he's paid to do – *manage.*

Taking things a stage further, the manager who con-templates dismissing an employee for incapability would be well advised to heed the lessons of history. For instance, before tumbling to its early demise, the National Industrial Relations Court provided us all with a salutary precedent:

If an employee is not measuring up to the job, it may be because he is not exerting himself sufficiently, or it may be because he really lacks the capability to do so. An employer should be very slow to dismiss upon the ground that the employee is incapable of performing the work which he is employed to do without first telling the employee of the respects in which he is failing to do his job adequately, warning him of the possibility or likelihood of dismissal on this ground and giving him an opportunity of improving his performance.

James v Waltham Holy Cross UDC (1973) ITR 467.

Safety first and good management is the key

Let's face it, in our hearts, we all know what has to be done – but, just in case, here is a checklist for your guidance when dealing with instances of incapability.

1   Once faced with indications of ailing performance, *be objective* – gather the *facts* of the case.
2   Present the facts to the employee, but *not* in the form of an indictment – and seek his or her reaction to your carefully worded, *constructive* criticism.
3   Discuss and agree with the employee ways and means of correcting the deficiencies – by relevant training, planned and supervised experience, etc.
4   Monitor (and that includes providing more than a smidgin' of encouragement) the employee's progress.
5   If, *after a reasonable period* (remember how easy it is to be *unreasonable* about this), the employee has failed to reach a satisfactory level of improvement, conduct a full and fair investigation into the matter. Seek and consider the employee's explanation for the failure to improve.
6   Then, if the circumstances fully warrant such action, issue a formal warning (see below).
7   In the event that the employee still fails to come up to scratch within the period stated in the warning, do not even consider dismissal unless or until the question of

Dismissing the baddies and the failures 123

NOTICE OF FORMAL WARNING

To **Miss I. M. Putrid**   *Job Title* **Warranty Clerk**

Dept **Service Dept**   *Date* **2 March 1988**

The purpose of this notice is to confirm that at a hearing held earlier today your performance as Warranty Clerk was deemed unsatisfactory; in that:

> despite your agreement during an interview held on 19 December 1987 that your standards of work in processing warranty claims were unacceptable, and notwithstanding your subsequent completion of a 7-day training course in warranty administration followed by a period of two weeks' supervised on-the-job experience, your overall performance has not reflected the required improvement.

After full consideration of this matter, you are now warned that your performance will be subject to further review on 1 May 1988, when any failure on your part to achieve a significant improvement during the interim perod will render you liable to dismissal without further warning. You have a right of appeal against this warning. If you wish to exercise this right, you should address your appeal, within seven days of the date of this notice, to the Service Director.

R. J. Harrap
Service Manager

I acknowledge receipt of a copy of this notice.

Signed .... Date .

Figure 13   *A typical warning in respect of incapability*

alternative, less demanding employment within the firm has been examined.

8   If dismissal is deemed necessary, ensure that this is implemented with notice, or pay in lieu of notice.

Please do not attach any particular significance to the dates (period of grace allowed, etc.) mentioned in Figure 13. I'm afraid the bad news is, you're very much on your own when it comes to deciding just how much latitude to allow in such matters; virtually all that the the legal pundits will offer in the way of help is that your decisions must be 'reasonable' in the light of the circumstances. You know, when a tribunal tsunami batters the average company edifice, all one can hear are agonised shrieks of, 'What in hell constitutes "*reasonable*"?'

When and if the question of dismissal for incapability looms its ugly head, remember, if you care for your bacon, that it should be dismissal with notice (or pay in lieu thereof). Figure 14 provides a skeleton example of the document required.

Dismissal for lack of qualifications

At first glance, you may be inclined to think that there's precious little difference between the terms 'incapability' and 'lack of qualifications', but there is. Dismissal on the latter ground is only likely to arise on the rarest of occasions; namely, when someone is employed on the contractual condition that he or she obtains a given qualification within a specified or reasonable period of time. If the employee fails to obtain the qualification (and provided that any conditional period of time *is* reasonable), then a tribunal would be likely to regard a consequent dismissal as fair.

Probation – the traditional let-out

Mention the word 'probation' to your average manager

Dismissing the baddies and the failures   125

NOTICE OF TERMINATION OF EMPLOYMENT

To .... *Job Title* ....

Dept .... *Date* ....

The purpose of this notice is to confirm that at a meeting held earlier today, you were adjudged incapable of achieving the required standards of performance in your present post and that, accordingly, your employment with this company

is terminated with immediate effect. Pay will be given in lieu of notice.*

will be terminated on .... The period of notice is for .... weeks.*

* Delete whichever is not applicable.

If you consider that your dismissal is wrongful or unfair, you have the right to appeal. If you wish to exercise this right, you should address your appeal in writing, within three working days of the date of this notice, to the ....

Signed ....

Appointment ....

(Manager authorizing dismissal)

Signed ....

(Employee being dismissed)

Figure 14   *Example of skeleton dismissal notice for incapability.*

126 The Secrets of Successful Hiring and Firing

(present company excepted, of course) and, as already mentioned, it's more than likely that the wily so-and-so will respond thus:

> 'Grow up, do – who in blazes is worried about probation? If you know your stuff, Goodworth, you ought to realize that, these days, the law allows us to have every blinkin' employee on probation. . . . Isn't it two years before anyone can complain of unfair dismissal? And what's that, if it isn't probation? I mean, there's no sweat – just kick 'em out before the two years are up, and you're as safe as houses. . . . Well, aren't you?'

Hum, I'd better put the record straight. . . . Thus far in these pages, I've made no mention of what the law terms 'employees who are excluded from the unfair dismissal provisions' – and there's a very good reason for this. Rightly or wrongly (and although I've made umpteen references to the law and industrial tribunals), I've assumed that you, reader, will wish to apply the principles of fair play 'across the board' – and that you'd be the very last person to think of committing dismissal skulduggery with those unfortunates who cannot complain. . . . Lest I am mistaken, and I jolly well hope I'm not, before dealing with the question of probation, here is a part-confirmation* on this wretched question of 'exclusions':

> Employees excluded from the unfair dismissal provisions are those who have not completed two years' continuous employment with the employer, or one year if starting with the employer before 1 June 1985 and the employer's organization employs more than 20 employees.
>
> Employment Protection (Consolidation) Act 1978 ss. 64(1) & 64A.

---

* But beware, where excluded employees are concerned, the EP(C)A 1978 does contain sundry other provisions – so do read them up.

Now, back to probationary service. . . . Provided an employer makes it clear at the time of recruitment that an employee is contractually required to serve a period of probation, then the employee bears some responsibility for establishing his suitability for the job concerned. Plainly, there is another side to the coin, in that the boss is responsible for ensuring that the employee has a fair crack of the whip in terms of training and discussions on progress. It goes without saying that the scrupulous employer will deal with instances of probationers' incapability in precisely the same manner as he would for any other members of his flock.

Incapability through ill-health
By any standards, this is a thorny issue and I reckon I can do no better than offer for your consideration what the Employment Appeals Tribunal has said on the subject:

> *Unless there are wholly exceptional circumstances before an employee is dismissed on the ground of ill-health it is necessary that he should be consulted and the matter discussed with him, and that in one way or another steps should be taken by the employer to discover the true medical position. We do not propose to lay down detailed principles to be applied in such cases, for what will be necessary in one case may not be appropriate in another. But if in every case employers take such steps as are sensible according to the circumstances to consult the employee and to discuss the matter with him, and to inform themselves upon the true medical position, it will be found in practice that all that is necessary has been done. Discussions and consultations will often bring to light facts and circumstances of which the employers were unaware, and which will throw new light on the problem. Or the employee may wish to seek medical advice on his own account, which, brought to the notice of the employers' medical advisers, will cause them to change their opinion.*

128   The Secrets of Successful Hiring and Firing

> *There are many possibilities. Only one thing is certain, and that is that if the employee is not consulted, and given an opportunity to state his case, an injustice may be done.*

East Lindsey DC v Daubney (1977) IRLR 181.

While, obviously, it is advisable for any employer wishing to check on the nature of an employee's ill-health (and, of course, the prognosis, in terms of the person's suitability for continued employment) to take the common step of enlisting the aid of his medical advisers, this should always be done with care. For instance, if it is considered desirable that the employee undergoes an examination by the company doctor, the employer can only *invite* the employee so to do. In the event that the man or woman declines such an invitation, that's that – except to add that any subsequent tribunal might well attach significance to the motives for the refusal.

By the way, the Employment Appeals Tribunal has reminded us of the positive greyness of this area of dismissal:

> *The decision to dismiss or not to dismiss is not a medical question, but a question to be answered by the employers in the light of the available medical advice. It is important therefore that when seeking advice employers should do so in terms suitably adjusted to the circumstances. Merely to be told . . . that an employee 'is unfit to carry out the duties of his post and should be retired on the grounds of permanent ill-health', is verging on the inadequate, because the employer may well need more detailed information before being able to make a rational and informed decision whether to diosmiss.*

Again, East Lindsey DC v Daubney (1977) IRLR 181.

Here is a checklist for handy use when deciding whether to dismiss a sick employee:

Dismissing the baddies and the failures 129

- have I kept in regular touch with the employee to check on his progress – and have I intimated that he or she may have to be replaced?
- Has a reasonable period of time passed since I intimated thus – and/or do I need to give a further, formal warning?
- Have I obtained advice from the company doctor and/ or, through him, an independent specialist's opinion regarding the employee's medical suitability for continued employment?
- Have I conducted a full and fair investigation into the case? Has the employee had more than half a chance to put his or her side of the matter?
- Have I considered the question of alternative employment within the company for this person?
- Would an independent observer agree with my conviction that, all things considered, I cannot be expected to wait any longer for this employee to return to work?
- If the case is one of frequent short absences due to so-called 'sickness', would there be a favourable response from the employee if I issued a formal warning regarding his/her totally unacceptable attendance record? (This ruse – for ruse it is – and the associated realization that dismissal is in the offing, sometimes jerks an employee into seeing sense.)

A touch of 'physician, heal thyself'

One of the penalties of management life is the ice-cold fact that there'll always be a number of rotten apples in every employment barrel; those couldn't-care-less, misconducting, scrimshanking creatures who'd drive any decent manager to distraction – and who merit nothing less than a merciless stroke of the dismissal axe. That said (and here comes the homily), there are also some pretty maggoty apples in the management basket – lousy caricature-like bosses and mini-bosses who wouldn't recognize justice if it smacked them between the eyes.

Don't be one of them.

8 Redundancy
The saddest cut of all

I suggest we kick off by reminding ourselves of the obvious. . . . No matter how much we shroud the wretched topic in platitudes, redundancy is just another form of dismissal – but, this time, it's the innocent who suffer. Point taken? Right, then let's proceed to a bit-by-bit examination of the procedure for handling redundancies.

1 GETTING TO GRIPS WITH THE BASIC DEFINITION OF REDUNDANCY

The law is pretty explicit on this one. It tells us that a dismissed employee is redundant if the dismissal is wholly or largely attributable to the fact that:

- the employer has ceased, or intends to cease:
  - (a) To carry on the business for the purposes of which the employee was employed by him; or
  - (b) To carry on the business in the place where the employee was so employed;

  or

- The requirements of the business for employees:
  - (a) to carry out work of a particular kind; or
  - (b) To carry out work of a particular kind in the place where the employee was employed;

134　*The Secrets of Successful Hiring and Firing*

have ceased or diminished, or are expected to cease or diminish.

Employment Protection (Consolidation) Act 1978 s. 81[2].

So, if you are in the unfortunate position of contemplating any redundancies, make absolutely certain that each one falls within this all-important definition.

2   THE DUTY TO AVOID REDUNDANCIES

Do you remember that word, 'reasonable'? Not surprisingly, it crops up with regular frequency in the law reports on redundancy cases – as, indeed, does its counterpart, the word, 'fair'; for example:

An employer's duty is to be fair both to the employee and to the business in all circumstances.

James v Waltham Holy Cross UDC (1973) IRLR 202.

Not to put too fine a point on it, you should make every reasonable effort to seek an alternative to redundancy; for example, by examining the possibilities of:

(a)　Retraining the folk concerned for alternative employment within your organization; and/or

(b)　Reducing the level of overtime; and/or

(c)　Introducing short-time working – which, albeit an unpleasant prospect, will be viewed by many as infinitely better than the sack.

What's that? Ah, yes, too true, you have also to be fair to your business – but are you *quite certain* that, in laying your plans, the scales are not unduly tipped in favour of your organization? If it came to the crunch, would an industrial tribunal support your view?

3 WHO IS ENTITLED TO A REDUNDANCY PAYMENT?

Broadly speaking, any employee who is dismissed for redundancy (including a volunteer) will be entitled to a redundancy payment provided that he or she has completed two years' continuous service, but excluding any week of service prior to the employee's eighteenth birthday. Since, however, this business of entitlement to a redundancy payment is hedged about with a near-plethora of 'ifs and buts', your golden rule in every case should be to telephone the local office of the Department of Employment for guidance.

4 THE REQUIREMENT TO CONSULT TRADE UNIONS

Employers are under a legal obligation to consult appropriate trade unions about proposed redundancies at the earliest opportunity – and, doubtless, mindful of just how tardy some employers are wont to be in this respect, the law prescribes a minimum time where groups of more than ten employees are concerned:

- If it is proposed to dismiss 10 to 99 employees as redundant at one establishment over a period of 30 days or less – *consultation must begin at least 30 days before the first dismissal takes effect.*
- If it is proposed to dismiss 100 or more employees as redundant at one establishment over a period of 90 days or less – *consultation must begin at least 90 days before the first dismissal takes effect.*

Employment Protection Act 1975 s.99(3).

Do remember that while the Act doesn't stipulate a minimum time for less than ten employees, those words, 'at

136 *The Secrets of Successful Hiring and Firing*

the earliest opportunity' do *not* mean that consultation can be left until the flamin' eve of execution.

Making fulsome use of the belt-and-braces principle, the good old law goes on to list the various titbits of information that employers must disclose in writing to the unions at the outset of consultation:

- The reasons for his proposals.
- The numbers and descriptions of employees whom it is proposed to dismiss as redundant.
- The total number of employees of any such description employed by the employer at the establishment in question.
- The proposed method of selecting the employees who may be dismissed.
- The proposed method of carrying out the dismissals, with due regard to any procedure, including the period over which the dismissals are to take effect.

Employment Protection Act 1975 s.99(5).

Note: We'll be looking at methods of selecting employees for redundancy later on.

Incidentally, the requirement to consult trade unions about proposed redundancies doesn't let the employer off the hook where individual employees are concerned:

We do not consider that it can be said that any reasonable employer is entitled to infer that an individual employee is privy to the negotiations that may take place between an employer and a trade union before a decision is made or an agreement is reached in relation to redundancy.

Huddersfield Parcels Ltd v Sykes (1981) IRLR 115.

They're your employees, not the union's – so keep them fully in the picture!

Catering as it does for nearly every contingency, the law

Redundancy 137

acknowledges that there may well be special circumstances where it is not reasonably practicable for an employer to go along with the requirements for minimum consultation periods – or, for that matter, the manner of dealing with the union's undoubted representations. In such cases, it is up to the boss to demonstrate that he is doing all he can reasonably be expected to do to match up to the requirements.

5 AND WHAT ABOUT CONSULTATION IN 'NON-UNION' SITUATIONS?

Reader, if we're going to fall out anywhere along this rickety line, it's more than likely that it'll be right now – but, for all that, here goes. Show me a bunch of 'non-unionized' companies and, redundancy-wise, I'll show you more than a few of them who are perfectly happy to drive a corporate horse and cart through the principles of fair play. Consultation at the earliest opportunity? You must be joking. . . .

> The scene . . . *A back office at Squidgems Ltd. A group of employees have been summoned to the presence of A Fall-Guy, Esq., Manager. Eyeing the uneasy figure with well-founded suspicion, they wait for him to speak.*

> Fall-Guy   (*Swallows hard*) 'Er, g'day. . . . I've, um, asked you here this morning because, er, following a lot of thought, we've. . . . (*Gives a nervous cough*) 'What I mean is, as you all know, there's a recession on and, er, – well, the fact is, I'm, um, sorry to tell you that you're all, er, redundant. . . .' (*Taking a deep breath, he hastens to complete Big Daddy's dirty work*) 'Now, I'm sure you'll agree that these things are best when they're, er, over and done with – so I'd like

138 *The Secrets of Successful Hiring and Firing*

> you to, um, get your personal belongings together and, Tompkins, here. . . .' (*Indicates a hapless side-kick*) '. . . will escort you to the, er, door.' (*Turns on a sickly smile*) 'And, er, thank you very much for all that you've, um, done – and, yes, you can collect your, er, redundancy money and what-not from Maisie on the way out. . . .'

No more facetiousness – you know it and I know it. For no other reason than they're scared witless what their unfortunate people may say or do, many such cowardly bosses ignore the need for consultation – and keep their mouths shut until the dawn of the fateful day, itself. To hell with telling them at the earliest opportunity that redundancy is in the offing, the need for hiccup-free work is all that matters. . . . After all, there's always the excuse that the situation didn't become clear until the last possible moment, isn't there?

The fact is, there are relatively few redundancy situations when it is genuinely impossible to provide at least some advance warning to the employees concerned. Of course, they're liable to be highly upset at the news, but they'll also respect the employer who does give them some time in which to draw breath – particularly if he is seen to be making every possible effort to find alternative solutions to redundancy.

6 NOTIFYING THE DEPARTMENT OF EMPLOYMENT

It shouldn't come as too much of a surprise to learn that employers are legally required to notify the Department of Employment whenever they plan to make ten or more employees at one establishment redundant within a given period. Far from being yet another example of government red tape, the process is necessary in order that the various manpower services not only keep their finger on the thumping pulse of unemployment, but are also enabled to lend help in terms of advising, retraining or even redeploying the people concerned. In this context, it's worth noting that many local authorities have special industrial units which provide a valuable advisory service to employers, particularly in cases where the proposed redundancies are of a hefty nature.

For administrative convenience, the minimum periods for notification are exactly the same as those governing advance warning and consultation with trade unions; i.e.:

- If it is planned to dismiss 10 to 99 employees as redundant at one establishment over a period of 30 days or less – *then notification must be made at least 30 days before the first dismissal takes effect.*
- If it is planned to dismiss 100 or more employees as redundant at one establishment over a period of 90 days or less – *then notification must be made at least 90 days before the first dismissal takes effect.*

Notification has to be made in writing and, needless to add, the government machine has a special form for the purpose – HR1, obtainable from any local DoE office.

There is, of course, the usual escape clause. If there are special circumstances where it isn't reasonably practicable for an employer to comply fully with the notification requirements, provided he does all that can reasonably be expected to meet the requirements, the DoE will usually accept his explanation.

7 THE THORNY BUSINESS OF SELECTION

While many employers have agreed procedures for redundancy selection, it's a fact that there are myriad organizations

140 *The Secrets of Successful Hiring and Firing*

(your's among them?) where no such formal arrangements exist. It's also a fact that, apart from having a notion that there's some general principle of 'last in, first out', the latter horde of employers are pretty ill-equipped when it comes to negotiating the selection minefield.

Now, the much-bandied phrase 'last in, first out' is all very well – but, when faced with the task of selecting one employee instead of another, length of service is only one of several factors which an employer should take into account. When you, reader, are next in this invidious position, ask yourself the following questions:

- All right, it's first on the list – who, of the two employees, *does* have the longest service?
- How do I rate each employee's capability and perform-ance – in as *near-objective* terms as possible?
- Who represents the most valuable asset in terms of relevant experience?
- And qualifications?
- Who comes off best in terms of conduct?
- Which of the two enjoys the best attendance record?
- Will one of them volunteer for redundancy?
- In considering the pros and cons, am I avoiding any form of discrimination on the grounds of sex, marital status or race (or, in Northern Ireland, sex or religion)?
- And, just in case I've forgotten the seriousness of such transgressions, am I avoiding any selection on the grounds of membership or non-membership of a trade union?

With all the above in mind, I cannot stress enough that the initial step must always be an in-depth consideration of how to *avoid* redundancies, not selecting people for it.

As a parting shot, the wise employer will go about his redundancy selection with one further thought always in mind:

Try as I might, this redundancy could be the one that lands me in front of a tribunal. If this did come about, am I as certain as I can be in the light of all the circumstances that my actions would be regarded as reasonable?

Remember the immutable provisions of Sod's Law – and don't take chances.

8 TIME OFF FOR JOB HUNTING OR TO ARRANGE TRAINING

Qualified employees (see note 3) who are given notice of dismissal on grounds of redundancy are legally entitled to *reasonable* time off with pay during their period of notice in order to seek alternative employment, attend job interviews or arrange training for alternative employment. Once again, it's down to the poor old boss to whip out the crystal ball and divine exactly what constitutes 'reasonable' time off for such activities.

The gristly bit in this particular sandwich is that failure by an employer to give reasonable time off with pay can land him in front of – yes, you've guessed it, an industrial tribunal. Employees who are thus unreasonably refused time off have a right to be paid the amount they would have been entitled to receive had they been allowed time off, subject to a limit of two-fifths of a week's pay. All right, such an order for compensation might not break the bank, but do give a thought to the likely adverse publicity involved. . . .

9 PUTTING PEN TO PAPER

For my sins, since the law on 'paid' redundancy first appeared (the Redundancy Payments Act 1965), I've had occasion to view many and various copies of associated

142 The Secrets of Successful Hiring and Firing

dismissal letters written by managers – and felt positively outraged at the tone in which some of these missives were couched. Plainly, the writers concerned attached little or no importance to the vital business of injecting sympathy or, for that matter, any other evidence of a caring attitude into their handiwork – and, sad to relate, the failing still persists. In all probability, the average manager's dislike (which, in

---

Dear ....

Confirming our discussion of earlier today, it is with much regret that I must ask you to accept this letter as formal notice of your dismissal from this company's service on the ground of redundancy with effect from . . . .

If you so wish, you may leave your employment on . . . , in which event you will be paid £ . . . as compensation in lieu of the pay during your period of . . . notice to which you are otherwise entitled under your contract of employment. If, however, you wish to work throughout the period of your notice, the company will be glad to allow you reasonable time off with pay for the purpose of seeking alternative employment, attending job interviews or arranging training for your future employment. Please let me have your decision in writing by . . . .

The services of the Personnel Department will, of course, be available to assist you in obtaining suitable, alternative employment. However, please do not hestitate to speak to me in the event that I can be of any help.

On behalf of the company, I should like to thank you for your loyalty and good service over the past years and wish you every success for the future. Needless to add, I shall be only too pleased to furnish any prospective employer with a reference on your behalf.

Your sincerely

Figure 15 *A skeleton letter of dismissal on redundancy*

many cases, almost amounts to a dread) of penning a formal letter is a root cause of some of the ill-worded, sterile and rotten efforts that emerge – but this is no excuse. If, perchance, you have difficulty in this vital area, for goodness sake do something about it – and, if necessary, mould the example at Figure 15 to your own specific requirements.

10   IN CASE OF EMERGENCY . . .

In the event that you have difficulty resolving any queries on redundancy with your local Job Centre or other Department of Employment office, it may be reassuring to know that there are 'specialist' DoE redundancy payments offices dotted throughout the country. They are located as follows:

Eastern Region
Hanway House
27 Red Lion Square
London WC1R 4NH
Tel: 01-405-8454

2–16 Church Road
Stanmore
HA7 4AW
Tel: 01-954-7588

Triton House
St Andrew's Street North
Bury St Edmunds
IP33 1TL
Tel: 0284-63121

Southern Region
12 Southey Road
London SW19 3RT
Tel: 01-542-5681

2nd Floor
New Oxford House
1 Station Road
Reading RG1 1LG
Tel: 0734-583411

Merevale House
42 London Road
Tunbridge Wells
TN1 1DN
Tel: 0892-39179

Midlands Region
2 Duchess Place
Hagley Road
Birmingham
B16 8NS
Tel: 021-455-7111

Commercial House
Thurland Street
Nottingham
NG1 3DR
Tel: 0602-411081

South West Region
The Pithay
Bristol
BS1 2NQ
Tel: 0272-21161

Yorkshire and Humberside Region
City House
New Station Street
Leeds
LS1 4JH
Tel: 0532-438232

North West Region
25 Aytoun Street
Manchester
M60 7HS
Tel: 061-236-4433

Red Rose House
Lancaster Road
Preston
PR1 1NS
Tel: 0772-21981

Newcastle Region
Wellbar House
Gallowgate
Newcastle upon Tyne
NE1 4TP
Tel: 0632-327575

Scotland Region
Pentland House
47 Robb's Lane
Edinburgh
EH14 1UE
Tel: 031-443-8731

146 *The Secrets of Successful Hiring and Firing*

Wales Region
Companies House
Crown Way
Maindy
Cardiff
CF4 3UW
Tel: 0222-388588

UNFAIR DISMISSAL FOR REDUNDANCY – A SUMMARY

In drawing the redundancy strings together, as it were, it's necessary to consider the number of sins which an unthinking or wilfully bad employer can commit – and which can result (surprise, surprise) in his being taken to the tribunal cleaners. The list of grounds for complaint of unfair dismissal for redundancy is formidable:

- A dismissed employee may complain that his job was not redundant (refer to note 1 for the definition of redundancy) – that, in fact, it still exists. The boss who uses redundancy as a method of ridding himself of an unwanted employee (i.e., as a deliberate ruse) is bucking for trouble, even if he has devoted some crooked energy to camouflaging the true state of affairs. The oft-heard, smug comment, 'Oh, of course, it's okay – all one's got to do is change the job title, and it's in the bag', has been a prelude to disaster for quite a few rascally employers.

- Another complaint may be that a dismissed employee was unfairly selected for redundancy – that, for some reason or other, an arbitrary decision was made without due regard for fair play (refer to note 7). In such instances, it is often the case that a 'blue-eyed boy' is retained – to the detriment of a less favoured employee who receives an undeserved and wholly unfair bullet.

Redundancy 147

- A dismissed employee may complain that there has been a failure by the employer to consult him at all, or to consult him adequately (refer to note 5) – or, for that matter, a failure to consult his recognized trade union (refer to note 4).
- Horror of horrors, a dismissed employee may complain that he was made redundant as a direct result of his membership, or non-membership, of a trade union. If this type of complaint is upheld by a tribunal, the employer had better get his piggy-bank out – because he's certainly going to need it. . . .
- A complaint may be that an employer selected the employee for redundancy in direct contravention of an agreed procedure – when, in fact, there were no special reasons to justify such an action in his case.
- A dismissed employee may complain that the employer failed to make any reasonable attempt to find him alternative employment within the organization (refer to note 2).
- Whoops, a dismissed employee may complain that his selection for redundancy was on the basis of, or influenced by, questions of sex, marital status or race.

In addition to the above possibilities, any questions relating to the right of an employee to a redundancy payment, or to the amount of any such payment, are referable to an industrial tribunal.

All in all, a pretty sinister minefield, I think you'll agree.

Let me round off this chapter by expressing the hope that you are never faced with the unpleasant task of making people redundant. If, however, such a day does dawn – well, my second and even more fervent hope is that you act fairly and reasonably. Think on it, it could be *your* turn next.

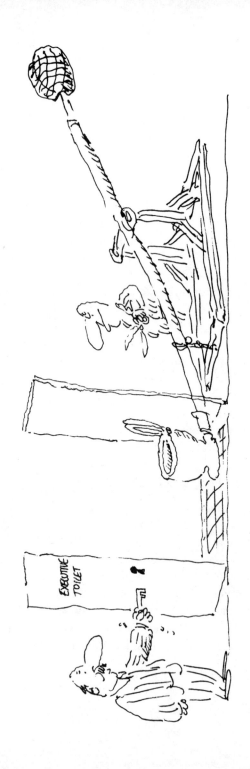

9 Dismissal hiccups and treading the tribunal trail

Beware the jabberwock, my son!

The preceding three chapters have been devoted, if you like, to the avoidance of complications when wielding the dismissal axe – which is just as it should be. If, however, your luck is anything like mine, try as you might, the time will come when glimmers of trouble heave up on the horizon – and you'll need to take some pretty cogent action if you're to prevent them bursting into flame. So, get your helmet on, for this final chapter is all about fire-fighting.

WRITTEN STATEMENTS OF REASONS FOR DISMISSAL

Some employers would have it (and, who knows, not without justification) that British employment law is rather like a nightmare – in that, just when you've had enough and your fevered brain is stirring you to wakefulness, along comes another ravening monster. . . . Although the provisions of the Employment Protection (Consolidation) Act 1978 relating to written statements of reasons for dismissal may not constitute a nightmare, they can cause the odd headache. Here goes with some aspirin!

Briefly, an employee who is dismissed, with or without notice, for any reason (including, mark you, an employee

150 *The Secrets of Successful Hiring and Firing*

whose fixed-term contract of employment is not renewed), has the legal right to be provided with a written statement of the reasons for his dismissal within 14 days of requesting the statement. There is, however, the important qualification that this chunk of law only applies to employees who have six months' continuous service under their belts at the effective date of termination of their employment. If an employer unreasonably refuses or fails to provide a statement, or provides one which is inadequate or untrue, the ex-employee has the right of complaint to an industrial tribunal on this score, alone.

It may happen, of course, that you are faced with a request for a statement from an ex-employee who has already received full details of why he got the chop within his letter of dismissal – what then? Well, provided the letter *is* adequately detailed, you can take heart from the following:

> *The requirement of s.53 is that, once a request has been received, the employer* must, *within 14 days, provide* in writing *a statement from which can be read the particulars of the reasons for the dismissal. Provided the covering letter refers unambiguously to the earlier letter which had been sent to the employee giving the reasons for dismissal, and provided a copy of that letter is included by the employer, it is a sufficient compliance with this section.*
>
> *Kent County Council v Gilham and Others (1985) IRLR 16 (Court of Appeal).*

Very typically, the law doesn't prescribe a set format or list the required contents of a statement of reasons for dismissal, but Mary-Lou and Joe Manager can't go far wrong if they proceed along the following lines:

● Employer's name – obviously, your company's letterhead will suffice for this purpose.

Dismissal hiccups and treading the tribunal trail 151

- Particulars of the ex-employee – name, job title, section or department.
- The effective date of termination of the employment.
- The important bit – the statement of reasons for the dismissal (of which more in a tick).
- Date of the statement and a signature on behalf of the employer.
- A space for the ex-employee's signature on a duplicate copy, together with the request that this is returned to the employer as evidence of receipt.

Bearing in mind the paramount need for accuracy and adequacy, I suggest that the 'reasons' chunk of the statement should utilize whichever of the following alternatives is appropriate:

- You were dismissed due to your gross misconduct; in that on (*date of the offence*) you (*concise details of the offence*), an offence for which you were adjudged guilty (*or* which you admitted) at a disciplinary hearing held on (*date*). The final stage of your appeal against this decision was heard by (*name and job title of manager concerned*) on (*date*) and, after due consideration, your dismissal was confirmed.
- You were dismissed due to your misconduct; in that on (*date of the offence*) you (*concise details of the offence*), an offence for which you were adjudged guilty (*or* which you admitted) at a disciplinary hearing held on (*date*). (*Add if relevant*) As you are aware, your previous warning for misconduct, dated (*date*), was taken into account at this hearing.) The final stage of your appeal against this decision was heard by (*name and job title of manager concerned*) on (*date*) and, after due consideration, your dismissal was confirmed.
- You were dismissed due to your lack of capability in performing work of the kind for which you were employed; in that, despite a warning dated (*date*) and

(*concise details of period of training, supervised experience, etc*), and as determined at a hearing held on (*date*), your performance (*or* standards of work) failed to reflect the required improvement. The final stage of your appeal against this decision was heard by (*name and job title of manager concerned*) on (*date*) and, after due consideration, your dismissal was confirmed.

- Your dismissal was due to your redundancy; in that the company's requirements for work of the kind for which you were employed (i.e., [*provide details of the duties concerned*]) have ceased (*or* diminished to the point where your job is no longer viable) (*or* are expected to cease) (*or* are expected to diminish to the point where your job is no longer viable).

- Your dismissal was due to the termination of your temporary (*or* fixed-term) contract of employment, in that the company's requirements of the nature for which you were temporarily employed (*or* employed on a fixed-term contract) have now ceased (*or, if relevant* because of the lack of need on the part of the company for the post to continue to be occupied by a temporary employee).

THE DODGY OLD BUSINESS OF REFERENCES

Many moons ago, while squatting at a personnel desk, I sent the traditional request for a reference to one job applicant's last employer – and duly received what I shall always regard as a memorable reply:

Dear Mr Goodworth

Not bloody likely!

Yours sincerely

So-and-so
Personnel Manager

Dismissal hiccups and treading the tribunal trail 153

While I can't exactly recommend this guy's approach, I have to admire his expressive brevity – which, at the time, had me picking up the telephone within seconds. Apropos of nothing, it rapidly became clear that I had come within an ace of recruiting a veritable Al Capone. . . .

All of which merely serves as an introduction to this section on references. So, no more mucking about, let's start off by disposing of the legal implications:

- First, the good news – there's no obligation whatsoever for any employer to supply a reference, however emphatically a request may be couched. Now the obvious, not-so-good news – the boss who refuses as a matter of principle to come up with the goods is, of course, condemning all his ex-employees to be labelled as potential baddies, and that is distinctly ropey.
- Aha, and here we're concerned with the stinker-type referee – the employer who supplies a reference which is false in some or other material particular. If it is subsequently established that the false statement has damaged the subject's reputation, then the employer may well be clobbered for *defamation* – or, in the case of simple lack of care on the employer's part, *negligent misstatement*.
- And we're not finished yet, me bucko. If it can be proved that an employer made a false statement in a reference with the object of persuading the recipient to take a certain course of action (like rejecting the subject's application for employment), then that employer stands in danger of being done for *deceit*.

With the above in mind, the wise old owl of an employer will always take care to include in his write-ups some sort of rider like: '*Please note that this reference is given without legal responsibility*'.

In writing this stuff, and because it's within the 'firing' part of the book, I'm tending to assume that you'll be on the

154 *The Secrets of Successful Hiring and Firing*

receiving-end of requests for references – which, as we all know, is only one half of the story. Maybe, therefore, it's wise to stress one golden rule which applies to both sides of the fence:

Whenever possible, conduct your reference business on the telephone.

Okay, I admit that it's not unknown for a wily ex-employee to get a pal to ring his old boss and, posing as a manager of some firm or other, ask for a verbal reference – but, if you wish to be extra-cautious (and add to your telephone bill), you can always say you'll ring back. The fact is, people tend to speak more freely on the telephone and there's a much better chance that the truth will out.

For all that, employers the world over love to see things in writing, and I dare say that, however much you may agree that the telephone is the best medium, you'll still be faced with the task of committing references to paper. That said, we'd better take a look at the widespread practice of supplying what some folk call 'between the lines' references – the escalating art of indicating that an ex-employee is an arch-bastard, or whatever, by simply saying very little:

Dear Mr Postlethwaite

Thank you for your letter of 12 February. I now confirm that Mr B G Twatt was employed by this company from 16 January 1986 to 14 December 1987 as a Storeman.

Yours sincerely

I M Corshuss
General Manager

There's no doubt at all about that one, is there? The writing may not be on the paper, but it's certainly on the wall – Job-Applicant Twatt is either a total incompetent or a right villain. Of course, if Mr Corshuss had been a little less so, he could have added a further and helpful sentence:

If you would care to give me a ring, I should be pleased to discuss the matter further.

We must not overlook another growing practice in this business of obtaining references, and that's the requirement for the referee to complete a form of questionnaire – which is often quite detailed, with such sections as:

Did you find him/her:

Cooperative? ....

....

Honest? ....

....

Reliable? ....

....

Are you aware of any reason why this company should not employ him/her? If so, please provide details. ....

....

....

and so on.

If you send such questionnaires to referees, jolly good – for they're certainly effective in getting more fulsome results. If, however, you are on the receiving-end and you feel dubious about completing the thing, or even the odd section – well, remember that you're under no obligation to comply with the sender's request. In such a case, note that your inaction will only be construed one way – so be fair, if you feel bound to consign the subject of the reference to employment purdah, do it fulsomely and honestly by means of a telephone call. And if you're one of nature's worriers and you can envisage a dirty great tape recorder at the other end of the line, preface your indictment with the *caveat* that you are making your comments without legal responsibility.

What about that other pitfall, the Rehabilitation of Offenders Act 1974? As I'm sure you are aware, this is the

156 *The Secrets of Successful Hiring and Firing*

chunk of legislation that, among other things, prohibits us from mentioning a subject's 'spent convictions' within a reference. Ever merciful, the law provides that an offender who has not been imprisoned for more than 2½ years, is 'rehabilitated' when, after the date of conviction, he or she is of good conduct for a specified period of time. Fine, but to be on the safe side, you've got to be aware of the rehabilitation periods involved:

Rehabilitation period

For a sentence of imprisonment between 6 months and 2½ years:	10 years★
For a sentence of imprisonment of 6 months or less:	7 years★
For cashiering, discharge with ignominy or dismissal with disgrace from the armed forces★★	10 years★
For simple dismissal from the armed forces★★	7 years★
For detention★★	5 years★
For a sentence of borstal training	7 years
For a fine or other sentence (e.g., a community service order) for which no other rehabilitation period is prescribed	5 years★
For an absolute discharge	6 months
For a probation order, conditional discharge or bind over; and for fit person orders, supervisions orders or care orders under the Children and Young Persons Acts (and their equivalents in Scotland)	1 year, or until the order expires (whichever is the longer)
For detention by direction of the Home Secretary: From 6 months to 2½ years	5 years

Dismissal hiccups and treading the tribunal trail 157

From 6 months or less	3 years
For a detention centre order	3 years
For a remand home order, approved school order or attendance centre order	The period of the order and a further year after the order expires
For a hospital order under the Mental Health Acts	The period of the order plus a further 2 years after the order expires (with a minimum of 5 years from the date of conviction)

* The period is halved for persons who were under the age of seventeen when they were convicted.
** Types of military punishment.

Additional notes

1 Any of the above rehabilitation periods will be extended in instances where the convicted person was disqualified (say, from driving) for a longer period than the relevant rehabilitation period stated. Note, however, that if the conviction took place while the person is 'serving' a rehabilitation period for a previous offence, the period of the disqualification (but not the 5 years or the fine) will not have the result of extending the previous rehabilitation period (as described in note 2).

2 A conviction for an indictable offence *during* a period of rehabilitation for an earlier conviction will result in the person serving a 'new, overall' period of rehabilitation relevant to the later offence (i.e., the 'original' rehabilitation period may be extended). If, however, the later offence was non-indictable, the original rehabilitation period is not affected.

  To further complicate the thing, if the later conviction involves a sentence of more than 2½ years, the 'original' rehabilitation period will never end and, hence, the offences will never be 'spent' – for the simple reason that a sentence of more than 2½ years puts the person concerned outside the scope of the Act.

3 A sentence in respect of a breach of probation, conditional discharge or binding over will invoke the rehabilitation period relevant to the sentence, and will 'cancel out' the earlier rehabilitation period.

158   *The Secrets of Successful Hiring and Firing*

Well, there you are! The message must be, think very carefully about the Rehabilitation of Offenders Act before making mention of convictions within a reference.

And now it's into battle. . . .

FACING AN INDUSTRIAL TRIBUNAL – AND SURVIVING

More often than not, an employer's first, blockbuster-sized indication that he's teetering on the edge of the tribunal mincing machine is the receipt of his copy of the applicant's complaint (form IT 1, the dreaded Originating Application to an Industrial Tribunal) – together with a tersely worded letter telling him that he has 14 days in which to 'enter an appearance' to the proceedings. The oh-so-innocuous-looking buff envelope will also contain a copy of form IT 3, the Notice of Appearance by Respondent – which will constitute the vehicle for his initial and outraged screams of innocence (although I should hasten to add that the form does cater for the rarity of a boss who desires to plead 'guilty' from the outset). It's at this point that we'd better evolve an order of battle in preparation for the coming campaign.

Initial action on receipt of a complaint

The first thing to remember is that 14-day period of grace in which to compile and enter an appearance – for as the letter from the Secretary of the Tribunals will state, a failure to enter an appearance can result in the employer being debarred from attending the subsequent hearing. Funnily enough, if the Notice of Appearance is not returned within the prescribed time, the tribunal will regard this as an application by the employer for an extension to the time limit – but, be warned, it will only grant such an extension if the employer provides sound reasons why such a course of action is necessary. The nasty upshot of all this is that if the

Dismissal hiccups and treading the tribunal trail 159

employer doesn't come up with his response (either within the 14 days, or within any duly granted extension of time), the case will be heard in his absence – and if that happens, you don't need a vivid imagination to forecast the result. . . .

So, it's time for tactical checklist number 1:

- Does the gravity of the complaint warrant handing the entire caboodle over to the company solicitor for his attention? If so, it follows that the remainder of this chapter will assume a somewhat academic hue, for it is really directed at the employer who, for whatever reasons, decides to plough his own tribunal furrow.
- The Originating Application will only convey the bare bones of the ex-employee's complaint:

His personal details.
The details of his employment.
The particulars of the complaint, together with a brief description of the events and circumstances which, in sum, constitute the grounds for the complaint.

Bearing in mind that the employer is required to provide sufficient particulars of his grounds for resisting the complaint, can the Notice of Appearance be returned within the 14-day period? If not, he should proceed as follows:

(a) *When a delay is necessary for purely administrative reasons*, apply to the Secretary of the Tribunals for an extension, giving the reasons (e.g., a key manager may be away on holiday).

(b) *When a delay is necessary because the Originating Application contains insufficient information to permit an adequate response*:

  (i) Apply for an extension, quoting this reason.

  (ii) At the same time, make application to the Secretary of the Tribunals for an order requiring the applicant to furnish in writing further particulars of the grounds for his complaint, together with his supporting evidence. Obviously, the application should be supported with good reasons why the employer is unable to respond on the basis of the information in the Originating Application.

● Is the sum and substance of the complaint such that, after careful consideration of all the available information (including, of course, an appraisal of *his* actions in the matter), the employer is satisfied that there is 'no case to answer'? If so, he should apply to the Secretary of the Tribunals for a *pre-hearing assessment* of the case, when (if the application is granted) the tribunal will decide whether or not the applicant's case stands a reasonable chance of success by considering:

(a) The information and assertions contained in the Originating Application and the Notice of Appearance.
(b) Any further written representations by either party.
(c) Any oral arguments presented at the pre-hearing assessment by either party.

Plainly, it's for the employer to hope that a pre-hearing assessment will result in the applicant being notified that, in the tribunal's view, his case stands no reasonable chance of success. The encouraging news is, in such instances, the applicant will be warned that, if he persists in his right to have a full hearing, he may have costs awarded against him in the event that his complaint subsequently fails – and that, you may agree, is a powerful disincentive to proceed. Perhaps I should add the obvious point that it could be the *employer* who is

Dismissal hiccups and treading the tribunal trail 161

found to be wanting – in which case, he would be well advised to think in terms of a swift 'out of court' settlement.

Enter the Conciliation Officer, stage left

At some time during this initial flurry of action, the local Conciliation Officer will be supplied with copies of the Originating Application and Notice of Appearance – and, fulfilling his role of impartial adviser, he'll offer his services to both parties.

Now, reader, this is where it's necessary for me to be blunt – almost, you may feel in a tick, to the point of rudeness. . . . One way or another, over the years I've had a fair amount of dealing with employers and their tribunal troubles – and I'm sick to death of hearing various Big Daddies who've got themselves enmeshed in very sticky tribunal proceedings talk vehemently along such lines as:

'Look, Goodworth, I know full well we're on dodgy ground – but it's the principle of the thing that matters. . . . I'm damned if I'm going to let that disloyal son-of-a-gun get away with it. We'll fight him all along the line. . . . I don't care if we do have to pay compensation – you mark my words, we'll give the bugger a good run for his money.'

'Talk settlement, d'you say? What the hell d'you take me for – an idiot? If that girl wants trouble, I'm just the person to give it to her. . . .'

If, following a frank appraisal of the facts, an employer is convinced that right is on his side, then he has the best of reasons for proceeding to a tribunal hearing – provided, that is, he is prepared to pay the intangible yet often damaging costs of the publicity involved. But if his decision to press on is founded in motives of sheer damned cussedness or a refusal to admit that he's in the wrong – he's a brass-bound idiot and a scoundrel, to boot.

162 *The Secrets of Successful Hiring and Firing*

So, if and when the need arises and the Conciliation Officer is freely available to offer his impartial advice, for goodness sake listen to it. Let the dictates of common sense and fair play be your arbiters – and if you or your outfit has acted unreasonably in the matter of the dismissal (or whatever), then use the Conciliation Officer as a ping-pong ball go-between and negotiate a settlement, but quick. It's on the cards that the Conciliation Officer will tell you that the ex-employee is seeking £x compensation – and if, as is often the case, this appears to be exorbitant, then make a counter-offer. Incidentally, always cap such offers with those magic words 'without prejudice' – especially and obviously if you're overkeen on not admitting your guilt. . . .

It is, of course, possible to settle a case right up to the moment of the hearing. However, for the purposes of this grim exercise, we'll assume that you have every just reason why the case should proceed – so let's do just that, proceed.

Preparing for the fray

Once the initial dust has settled and the notified date of hearing is something more than an indistinct blob on the horizon, it's likely that thoughts will return to the question of whether it would be better to employ legal represent-ation. Putting aside any question of the additional costs involved (and, dare it be said, the business of assuring oneself that one's company solicitor is suitably experienced in tribunal cases – which ain't always the happy case), there's one other factor which is worthy of consideration. As all the pundits tell us, tribunals are arbiters of fact – and it doesn't necessarily follow that brilliant legal expositions and references to precedent are what are wanted. Although it makes somewhat difficult reading, consider what the Employment Appeals Tribunal has said on the subject when referring to some past judgements:

Dismissal hiccups and treading the tribunal trail   163

Those cases have implicitly declared that the days are passing, if not already passed, when industrial tribunals were to be treated as dependent for the discharge of their fact-finding role upon judicial 'guidelines' sought to be extracted from reported decisions in other cases. Such dependency was understandable when the jurisdiction was in its infancy, but the Court of Appeal has now made it plain that for an industrial tribunal there can be no authority more persuasive than the language of Parliament. That must especially be so when Parliament has directed an appraisal of the 'reasonableness' of a particular decision or action. In the infinite variety of circumstances, it can never be right to constrain the criteria by which a person's conduct is judged. Sometimes the judgement in a particular case will be found to express, in concise and helpful language, some concept which is regularly found in this field of inquiry and it becomes of great illustrative value. But reference to such a case can never be a substitute for taking the explicit directions of the statute as the guiding principle.

The objective of Parliament, when it first framed the right not to be unfairly dismissed and set up a system of industrial tribunals (with a majority of lay members) to administer it, was to banish legalism and in particular to ensure that, wherever possible, parties conducting their own case would be able to face the tribunal with the same ease and confidence as those professionally represented. A preoccupation with guideline authority puts that objective in jeopardy. It should seldom be necessary (and may sometimes even be unwise) for an industrial tribunal to frame its decision by reference to any direction other than the express terms of the statute.

Anandarajah v Lord Chancellor's Department (1984) IRLR 131.

164 *The Secrets of Successful Hiring and Firing*

There it is, straight from the learned horse's mouth – and the lesson is, think carefully before deciding that a moderately proficient manager (especially a personnel manager) is incapable of conducting an able representation at a tribunal hearing. After all, there are a number of sources from which he or she can glean valuable advice: the library shelves; personnel-cum-industrial relations periodicals; the advisory services offered by employers' associations and professional institutions; and, to satisfy the glutton for punishment, the Industrial Relations Law Reports themselves.

All of which brings us to tactical checklist number 2.

● *Assemble the facts of the case – all of them.* While, doubtless, the requirement to enter a Notice of Appearance will have triggered off a somewhat frenetic gathering of the salient facts of the case (together with more than a few excursions into fancy), it is at this later and calmer stage that a microscopic appraisal of the situation should be carried out.

    (a)   *Who* are the witnesses as to fact?
    (b)   Precisely *what* does each witness have to say?
    (c)   Are their testimonies borne out by corroboration, documentary or other solid evidence?
    (d)   When considered as a whole, does each facet of the case 'dovetail' in logical fashion – or are there areas of weakness?
    (e)   Arising from this examination, how *exactly* does the case stand vis-à-vis the law?

● *Assemble the documentary evidence – every scrap.* Prepare what, in effect, is a dossier of all the necessary documents; including copies of:

    (a)   The applicant's letter of employment, written statement of particulars of employment/contract of employment, job description.

Dismissal hiccups and treading the tribunal trail   165

(b)   Any subsequent amendments to the above.

(c)   In cases of misconduct, all formal warnings and any other relevant letters or memos.

(d)   In cases of incapability, all formal warnings, records of training, appraisal reports, etc.

(e)   If relevant, the company's disciplinary procedure or published redundancy policy.

(f)   The applicant's letter/notification of dismissal.

(g)   If relevant, the statement of reasons for dismissal.

(h)   Evidence of the applicant's latest rates of pay and other emoluments.

● _Prepare an itemized list of the documentary evidence_ and send copies of this to the tribunal _and_ the applicant at least seven days prior to the date of the hearing.

● _Prepare seven sets of the documentary evidence._ Three sets are required to be presented to the tribunal at the opening of the hearing, together with two sets for the applicant and his representative, if any. The remaining two should be retained for personal use at the hearing.

It has been suggested that once the sets of evidence have been prepared, the applicant's copies should be forwarded to him – a form of gentlemanly gesture, if you like. If the applicant is represented, it is very likely that his representative will request that this be done as part and parcel of the process of 'agreeing bundles' – agreement between the parties prior to the hearing as to what each set of evidence will contain (an obvious time-saver).

● _Ensure that whoever is representing the company's case has a thorough knowledge of the evidence to be given by each of the witnesses._ One method of achieving this is to obtain written statements from each witness – but do note that witnesses may only be allowed to read from these statements at the hearing with the agreement of the other side _and_ at the ultimate discretion of the tribunal.

166   *The Secrets of Successful Hiring and Firing*

- *Make every effort to anticipate the applicant's case.* The discussion with the Conciliation Officer, albeit abortive, should have added a bit of flesh to the bare bones of his Originating Application. It is now vitally necessary to:

  (a) Evolve a prognosis of the manner in which his case will be developed and presented;

  (b) Arising from this prognosis, formulate a series of 'lines to be taken' in cross-examination of the other side's likely evidence;

  (c) Examine the company evidence and endeavour to anticipate how the other side will conduct *their* cross-examination.

The tribunal setting dissected

To most of us, the mere prospect of attending a tribunal hearing as a witness, let alone as a full-blown representative, is more than enough to precipitate a severe and lasting attack of the collywobbles. If one has never before set foot inside a court of law, one's imagination (and memories of Perry Mason and what-all) will likely create some fairly horrific conjectures of 'what it's going to be like' – and if one *has* suffered a previous court appearance, it could be even worse. . . . So, with the galloping gunkies of fear in mind, let's pay a cool-headed visit to a typical tribunal establishment – and view the redoubtable denizens of this legal lair.

On arrival, you'll find that separate waiting rooms are provided for use by the respondent (that's you, in case you've forgotten) and the applicant, wherein both parties sit and the addicted among them smoke like fury while awaiting the call to the tribunal.

However, we don't have to hang around – we can drift as unseen wraiths down the corridor and into the holy of holies. It's a largish room, simply furnished and decorated, with none of the traditionally sombre judicial trappings that

Dismissal hiccups and treading the tribunal trail 167

so intimidate the innocent, to say nothing of the guilty. True, at one end of the room, there's an inches-high platform with a run-of-the-mill table and chairs thereon – this mini-elevation of the worthy tribunal being the one and only sop to the majesty of the law. Facing the platform are tables and chairs for the use of the applicant and respondent; and, behind them, a few rows of chairs to accommodate any onlookers – for an industrial tribunal hearing is open to the public. In the 'well' of the room (or where the well would be if there was one), there are a couple of small tables and chairs – one for the use of witnesses and one for that ubiquitous fetcher-and-carrier, the clerk to the tribunal. Way back at the rear of the room, there's likely to be another table and chairs for use by the ladies and gentlemen of our fourth estate, the press. It is customary to find flasks of water and tumblers kindly provided for all the case participants – and that's about it. Not, I think you'll agree, a very daunting set-up. . . .

As we watch, the chairman and two lay members of the tribunal enter the room and seat themselves at their table. The chairman, a full-time employee of the tribunals, is required to be legally qualified – and is, therefore, either a solicitor or barrister by profession. One lay member is a person who, duly experienced in 'things management', has to have been recommended for this part-time post by an employers' organization – and the second lay member, duly experienced in 'the workers' side', has to have been recommended by an employees' organization, usually a trade union. Thus, we have it, the industrial tribunal – kept on the legal straight and narrow by the chairman, and tasked with reaching its many and various decisions by unanimous or majority vote.

The tenor of the proceedings
Surprisingly enough, there is no established procedure for a tribunal to follow when carrying out its business. In point

168 *The Secrets of Successful Hiring and Firing*

of fact, they are entirely free to conduct a hearing in the manner they deem most suited to the clarification and eventual resolution of the case concerned. Hence, there is a healthy accent on informality – notably, even to the extent that they're not slavishly bound by the Rules of Evidence. While most chairmen will, nevertheless, tut-tut if a representative indulges in too many leading questions, if the tribunal wishes to hear hearsay evidence or listen to opinion, then they can do so.

A further feature of this welcome informality is the fact that the chairman will usually bend over backwards to help a witness give evidence – particularly in the case of a nervous applicant who has decided to go it alone. This entirely laudable approach often provokes anguished screams from some employers, who protest that tribunals are thus biased in favour of the applicant – a piece of nonsense which is amply disproved by the statistics on tribunal decisions. Like it or not, there is a heap of difference between helping a moderately inarticulate and probably timid applicant to present his case, and actually helping him to win it – and, in practice, the latter just doesn't happen.

All of this should be good news for any newly-dubbed respondent – but, wait, there's more to come. For some deep reason which I've been unable to fathom (in truth, I haven't tried all that hard), the tribunal chairman is required to make copious longhand notes of all that transpires during a hearing, with the inevitable result that the entire caboodle is punctuated with lengthy pauses as the poor chap writes and writes like a demented novelist. Since this note-taking is also taking place during any episodes of cross-examination, it follows that the traditional cut-and-thrust and verbal slaughter so beloved of legal-beagles is wholly conspicuous by its absence – all cross-examination (and re-examination) proceeds at a lame snail's pace.

Legal-beagle (*Cross-examining a witness*) 'Mr Bloggs, please

Dismissal hiccups and treading the tribunal trail 169

	remember that you have taken the oath. . . . I wish to ask you. . . .'
Chairman	(*Interrupts*) 'Mr Blenkinsop, I'm sure that the witness remembers taking the oath – after all, it was only administered about three minutes ago, was it not?'
Legal-beagle	'Er, yes, sir. . . . Now, Mr Bloggs, during the morning of 4th May last, did you or did you not strike Mr Twatt, your manager, on the nose?'
Chairman	(*Writing busily*) 'One moment, if you please, Mr Blenkinsop.'
Legal-beagle	'Certainly, Mr Chairman. . . .' (*Drums fingers on table during a seemingly interminable pause*) 'Well, Mr Bloggs – did you?'
Bloggs	'Did I what?'
Legal-beagle	(*Very loudly*) 'Did you hit Mr Twatt on the nose – yes or no?'
Chairman	'Kindly refrain from raising your voice, Mr Blenkinsop. Now, Mr Bloggs, Mr Blenkinsop is asking whether or not, on the morning of, er . . .' (*Consults his notes*) '. . . 4th May, last, you struck Mr Twatt on the nose. What is your reply to that?'
Bloggs	'No, sir, I didn't.'
Legal-beagle	'I put it to you that you did!'
Chairman	(*Resignedly*) 'Mr Blenkinsop, the witness has just stated that he did not – do you really see any useful advantage in pressing the point? I have noted the witness's reply. . . .'
Legal-beagle	'Mr Chairman, I will be introducing evidence to the effect that the witness did so strike Mr Twatt on the nose, and. . . .'
Chairman	(*Interrupts smoothly*) 'And we will listen very carefully to any witness you produce, Mr Blenkinsop. Now, may we get on with it?'

Lega-beagle	(*Ruffled*) 'Mr Bloggs, I put it to you. . . .'
Chairman	(*Interrupts nastily*) 'No, no, no, Mr Blenkin-sop – you are not conducting a cross-examination at the Old Bailey. Be good enough to refrain from further "putting" – merely frame your questions as simply and succinctly as is necessary for the witness to understand them.'
Leagle-beagle	(*Now thoroughly out of sorts*) 'Mr Bloggs, if you did not hit Mr Twatt on the nose – why, pray, were you subsequently dismissed?'
Chairman	'One moment, please.' (*Again, writes busily*) Er, yes, Mr Bloggs?'
Bloggs	''Cos I hit him in the eye.'

Presenting and hopefully winning one's case

Since the tribunal is arbiter of its own affairs, the chairman will decide whether the applicant or the respondent will open the proceedings – but, whenever, the respondent has the choice of either kicking straight off with his first witness, or providing the tribunal with a short opening summary of the case he intends to present. The latter course is usually appreciated by the tribunal, provided that the summary *is* short.

Once each witness has taken the oath (or affirmed), he will either be invited by the chairman to tell his story at a moderate pace – or, if permission has been granted, read his statement. As implied earlier, most chairmen will not permit blatant leading of witnesses and this should be avoided. The chairman is likely to interject with a number of questions in order to clarify things in his mind – and, when the witness has finished his spiel, he will invite the lay members to pose any queries they may have.

It is then up to the applicant, or the applicant's represent-ative, to cross-examine each witness (of which, enough said), and this will be followed by the respondent's re-

Dismissal hiccups and treading the tribunal trail 171

examination – when he may seek to reinforce any weaknesses suggested or made apparent during the cross-examination.

When both sides have given their evidence, they may, if they so desire (and this is always advisable), present closing addresses to the tribunal. Needless to say, a closing address should be as telling and succinct as possible. Much of its content will be dictated by that which has transpired during the hearing, but it is always a good tactic to prepare a 'bare-bones' list of pointers in advance, particularly if one is taking refuge in any case precedent.

In many tribunal cases the decision will be announced by the chairman at the end of the hearing. However, in complex cases, the chairman may well announce that the tribunal has decided to reserve its decision for notification at a later date. If a decision is announced at the end of the hearing, and the complaint is upheld, then the tribunal will normally proceed immediately to the questions of any monetary award and/or reinstatement or re-engagement order deemed fit in all the circumstances.

As a parting shot, let me express my surprise at the horde of managers who scream like billy-o when they find themselves *required* to attend a tribunal hearing – and, yet, who've never taken the trouble to prepare for this increasingly likely event by visiting one as part-and-parcel of their general education. There's a tribunal near you, reader, so don't be an ostrich. . . . Get off your executive butt and find out what happens, for real – there's no better way to learn the tribunal ropes!

'Bye now, and have a good day.

Appendix 1 Examples of application forms

This appendix comprises two examples of application forms designed for use in the recruitment of:

(a) Clerical and other junior staff.
(b) Managers.

Reader, please note – bearing in mind that application forms should be tailored to suit the precise needs of the organization concerned, these examples are purely intended to serve as triggers for your own thoughts. So, get designing!

Appendix 1   173

CONFIDENTIAL

RAYLEIGH AERONAUTICS LTD

Vacancy for _____   Department _____

If you find there is insufficient space on this application form, please proceed to a separate sheet of paper. You should note that we will not approach any employers without your express permission.

PERSONAL DETAILS

Surname _____   Forenames _____

Address _____

_____

Tel no. _____   Date of birth _____

Detail any medical disabilities which could have a bearing on this application

_____

Date of last medical examination _____

If registered disabled, state Registration no. _____

EMPLOYMENT HISTORY (Last three employers)

From	To	Employers' name, address and telephone number	Job held and reason for leaving

Briefly describe your main duties and responsibilities in your current or last employment

EDUCATION

Dates		Name of school	Examinations – list *all* subjects taken and grades awarded
From	To		

Details of any school positions held (prefect, team captain, etc.)

FURTHER EDUCATION

Dates		Place of study	Details of course and results obtained
From	To		

HOBBIES AND OTHER LEISURE ACTIVITIES

Indicate the nature and depth of your involvement in each activity

PLEASE NOTE

This company is an equal opportunity employer. The aim of our policy is to ensure that no applicant for employment receives less favourable treatment on the grounds of race, colour, nationality, or ethnic or national origins, or is disadvantaged by conditions or requirements which have a disproportionately adverse effect on his or her racial group and which cannot be shown to be justifiable on other than racial grounds.

I certify that to the best of my knowledge the information I have provided in this application form is correct.

Signed _____ Date _____

CONFIDENTIAL

Name of applicant ....

Post applied for ....

RAYLEIGH AERONAUTICS LTD

Application for management appointment

Note to applicant Please do not hesitate to utilize a separate sheet of paper for any additional information deemed necessary.

PERSONAL DETAILS

Surname   Forenames

Address

Tel no.   Date of birth

DETAILS OF CURRENT/LATEST EMPLOYMENT

Employer's name and address   Your job title

Tel no.   Employment dates
                                    From   To

Nature of business

Name and appointment of person to whom you were directly
responsible

Brief details of his/her main duties and responsibilities

Brief details of your main duties and responsibilities

Appendix 1   177

Please indicate by means of a diagram
your position in the organization

Starting salary

Current/latest
salary

Other benefits

Please give your concise reasons for wishing to leave/leaving this
employment

What do you regard as your most outstanding achievement(s) in
this appointment?

Briefly describe what you regard as your *relative* strengths and
weaknesses in this appointment

Strengths

Weaknesses

178 *The Secrets of Successful Hiring and Firing*

PREVIOUS EMPLOYMENT HISTORY

Employer's name and address　　　　Your job title

Tel no.　　　　　　　　　　　　Employment dates
Nature of business　　　　　　　From　　　To

Brief details of your main duties and responsibilities

Please state your concise reasons for leaving this employment

Employer's name and address　　　　Your job title

Nature of business　　　　　　　Employment dates
　　　　　　　　　　　　　　　From　　　To

Brief details of your main duties and responsibilities

Reason for leaving

Appendix 1   179

Employer's name and address   Your job title

_____

Nature of business   Employment dates
                                  From   To

Brief details of your main duties and responsibilities

Reason for leaving

Employer's name and address   Your job title

_____

Nature of business   Employment dates
                                  From   To

Brief details of your main duties and responsibilities

Reason for leaving

The Secrets of Successful Hiring and Firing

Employer's name and address   Your job title

Nature of business   Employment dates
                                      From   To

Brief details of your main duties and responsibilities

Reason for leaving

QUALIFICATIONS AND MEMBERSHIP OF PROFESSIONAL BODIES, ETC.

List all professional, university and/or other examination qualifications gained since leaving school

Qualification/examination	Date	Place of study	Length of course and pass grade

Fee-paying membership of professional institutions, societies, etc

Name of body	Date	Grade of membership	Date of last subscription

Appendix 1 181

OTHER QUALIFICATIONS AND EXPERIENCE

Please detail any other qualifications and/or experience which you consider relevant to the post for which you are applying

EDUCATION

| Dates | | Name of school | Examinations – list *all* subjects taken and grades awarded |
| From | To | | |

Details of membership of any school societies/groups

Details of any official positions held (prefect, house/team captain etc.)

182   *The Secrets of Successful Hiring and Firing*

HOBBIES AND OTHER LEISURE ACTIVITIES

Please indicate the nature and depth of your involvement in each activity

PLEASE NOTE

This company is an equal opportunity employer. The aim of our policy is to ensure that no applicant for employment receives less favourable treatment on the grounds of race, colour, nationality, or ethnic or national origins, or is disadvantaged by conditions or requirements which have a disproportionately adverse effect on his or her racial group and which cannot be shown to be justifiable on other than racial grounds.

In the event that your application is successful, your appointment is subject to the receipt by the company of satisfactory employment references which will not normally be taken up until you have accepted our offer.

I certify that to the best of my knowledge the information I have provided in this application form is correct.

Signed _____   Date _____

Appendix 2 Example of a written statement of particulars of employment

RAYLEIGH AERONAUTICS LTD

STATEMENT OF PARTICULARS OF EMPLOYMENT

Name: Mr George Ian HARRAP

Date of commencement of employment: 1 June 1987

Date of issue of statement: 5 June 1987

1 You have been appointed to the post of Training Officer in the Personnel Department of this company.
2 Your duties and responsibilities will be as described in the attached job description, but this job description should not be regarded as exclusive or exhaustive. There will be other occasional duties and requirements associated with your post and, in addition, as a term of your employment, you may be required to undertake various other duties and/or hours of work as may be reasonably required of you.
3 The date of commencement of your continuous service with this company is 1 October 1985 (i.e., the date of your appointment as Training Assistant).
4 Your specific terms and conditions of employment are contained in the Employees' Handbook issued by the company, a copy of which is enclosed for your retention. The company undertakes that any further changes in your terms and conditions of employment will be notified to you within 30 days of such change.

184   *The Secrets of Successful Hiring and Firing*

5   Confirmation of your appointment as Training Officer will be subject to your satisfactory completion of 3 months' probationary service.

6   Your current salary is £11,800 per year. Your salary is paid monthly in arrears by credit transfer to the bank notified by you. Overtime is not payable.

7   Your normal working hours are 9.00 a.m. to 5.30 p.m. Monday to Friday.

8   Your entitlement to pay during periods of sickness is as outlined in Section 9(b) of the Employees' Handbook.

9   Your annual holiday entitlement is 20 working days.

10   The minimum periods of notice to which you are entitled are detailed in Section 10 of the Employees' Handbook.

11   Your position with regard to pension is set out in the explanatory booklet enclosed for your retention. There is a contracting-out certificate in force in respect of your employment.

12   You have a right to join a trade union and take part in its activities.

13   The disciplinary rules applicable to you are detailed in Section 12 of the Employees' Booklet. In the event that you wish to appeal against any disciplinary decision relating to you, you should apply to the next level of management concerned as specified in the Employees' Booklet.

14   In the event that you have a grievance relating to your employment, you should refer to the procedure detailed in Section 13 of the Employees' Booklet.

(Signed)
I D R Pringle
Personnel Manager

I acknowledge receipt of a copy of the above.

(Signed)
G I Harrap   Date: 5 June 1987

Recommended reading list

Advisory, Conciliation and Arbitration Service, *Advisory Booklet No. 6 – Recruitment and Selection*, ACAS, revised edition, 1984.

Department of Employment, *Employment Legislation – Series of Booklets*, a number of invaluable publications available free of charge from any DoE office.

Goodworth, Clive T., *Effective Interviewing for Employment Section*, 2nd ed., Business Books, 1983.

Green, G. D., *Industrial Relations*, 2nd ed., Pitman, 1987.

Hackett, P., Schofield, P. and Armstrong, M., *The Daily Telegraph Recruitment Handbook*, 2nd ed., New Opportunity Press and Kogan Page, 1982.

Higham, M., *The ABC of Interviewing*, Institute of Personnel Management, 1979.

Plumbley, Philip Rodney, *Recruitment and Selection*, Institute of Personnel Management, 1976.

Index

Application forms, design of:
  education history section, 25
  employment history section, 16
  examples of typical forms, App A
  hobbies/leisure interests section, 25
  legal constraints, 11
  medical questionnaires, 29
  qualifications section, 22
  referees section, 29

Capability and/or qualifications, dismissal for lack of:
  ill-health, through, 127
  introduction to, 119
  note regarding 'lack of qualifications', 124
  notice of formal warning for, 123
  notice of dismissal for, 125
  pre-dismissal checklist, 122
  probation, during, 124
Constructive dismissal, 104
Contracts of employment, 92
Disciplinary procedure, checking a, 102

Dismissal:
  capability and/or qualifications, for lack of, 119
  constructive dismissal, 104
  ill-health, incapability through, 127
  misconduct, for, 109
  reasonableness of action in, 101
  redundancy, 133

188　*Index*

suspension pending outcome of an investigation,　105
statutory minimum periods of notice,　104
summary dismissal,　103

Employee specifications, content of,　6

Incapability through ill-health, dismissal for,　127
Induction training,　94
Industrial tribunals in general:
　case preparation by employer,　164
　Conciliation Officer in cases, part played by the,　161
　initial action by employer on receipt of a complaint,　158
　presenting the employer's case,　170
　proceedings, tenor of the,　167
　setting and composition of,　166
Interviewing:
　direct questions,　78
　Five-fold-interview grading scheme,　76
　interview environment,　59
　invitation to attend for interview,　58
　open-ended questions,　77
　planning the interview,　75
　post-interview assessment procedure,　85
　questioning techniques,　77
　rejecting interviewed candidates,　87
　sample interview questions:
　　probing employment,　82
　　probing important requirements,　84
　　probing leisure activities,　83
　　probing schooling,　81
　　settling-in candidates,　80
　self-questionnaire on interviewing skills and aptitudes,　60
　standard revealing questions,　79
　Seven-point interview plan,　75

Job descriptions, content of,　5

Medical questionnaires,　29
Misconduct:
　pre-dismissal checklist,　119
　dismissal for,　109
　dismissal for 'totted-up' offences,　116
　notice of final warning for,　118
　notice of formal warning for,　117

Index 189

notification of summary dismissal for, 120
practical tips on dealing with gross misconduct, 113
questions and answers on, 110

Probation:
dismissal for lack of capability and/or qualifications, 124
from a recruitment aspect, 93

Qualifications and/or capability, dismissal for lack of, 119

Recruitment advertising:
aims of, 37
'box number' advertisements, 46
choosing the right publication, 44
describing the post, 38
enhancing the company image, 43
Equal Opportunity employment, 49
eradicating flannel, 39
obtaining an appropriate response, 37
phrase-bank for advertisements, 46
position of advertisements, 44
'salary negotiable' advertisements, 46
size of advertisements, 43
timing advertisements, 45
Recruitment and selection:
contracts of employment, 92
induction training, 94
internal recruitment, 33
interviewing techniques, 77
invitation to attend for interview, 58
offer of employment, 90
overall policy for, 8
probation, 93
recommendations from existing employees, 33
recruitment advertising, 37
recruitment documentation, 90
rejecting candidates not short-listed, 57
rejecting interviewed candidates, 87
short-listing, 53
sources of recruitment, 33
written statements of particulars of employment, 91
Redundancy:
basic definition of, 133

190 *Index*

Department of Employment, requirement to notify, 138
employees, requirement to consult with, 137
employer's duty to avoid, 134
handy addresses for advice on, 143
redundancy payments, 135
selection for, 139
time off work for job-hunting/arranging training, 141
trade unions, requirement to consult with, 135
unfair dismissal for, a summary on, 146
written notification to employee, 141
References:
in general, 152
and the Rehabilitation of Offenders Act 1974, 155
Rejecting candidates:
not shortlisted, 57
post-interview, 86

Self-questionnaire on interviewing skills and aptitudes, 60
Short-listing:
introduction to, 53
process of, 55
rejecting candidates not short-listed, 57
Sources of recruitment:
Job Centres, 35
Professional and Executive Register, 36
recommendations from existing employees, 33
recruitment advertising, 37
Statutory minimum periods of notice, 104
Summary dismissal, 103
Suspension from employment, 105

Written statements of particulars of employment:
and contracts of employment, 92
minimum details, 91
Written statements of reasons for dismissal:
example, App. B
format of, 150
introduction to, 149
sample skeleton statements, 151